Opening King David

Opening King David

Poems in Conversation with the Psalms

BRAD DAVIS

An *EMERALD CITY* Book

OPENING KING DAVID
Poems in Conversation with the Psalms

Resource Publications
An Imprint of Wipf and Stock Publishers
199 W. 8th Ave., Suite 3
Eugene, OR 97401

www.wipfandstock.com

ISBN 13: 978-1-60899-554-7

Manufactured in the U.S.A.

For Deb, John, and Mariko—and all who struggle and hope

These conjectures as to why God does what He does are probably of no more value than my dog's ideas of what I am up to when I sit and read.

—C. S. Lewis,
Reflections on the Psalms

Contents

BOOK TWO

BOOK THREE

BOOK FOUR

BOOK FIVE

Preface

THE WRITING OF THESE poems began on the first Sunday in Advent 2002. Over the next six years, they were drafted (sequentially through 2005) and then revised. The plan was to make a slow, contemplative read (*lectio divina*) through the Bible's book of Psalms, one psalm a week, and by each week's end to draft a poem in loose conversation with the biblical text. The intention was not to create a new translation/adaptation of the Psalms, engage in midrash, or even generate "religious" verse, but to make poems in a conversational idiom that bear witness to an attention to three horizons: the text, my surroundings (natural, cultural, relational, situational), and whatever may have been happening inside my skin at the time of composition. The sequence is an extended ekphrasis, writing that reflects upon and calls attention to another art form, in this case the 150 liturgical song lyrics of the biblical Psalter.

Other than to utilize a generally hospitable idiom (one of the rhetorical strategies in the Psalms), I set for myself no formal parameters though early on enjoyed working with a decasyllabic line and toward a sonnet-like fourteen-line form (in Book One especially) to which I returned here and there throughout the drafting process. Rhyme and regular rhythm happen now and then, but these are more happy accidents I decided to keep than anything else. Likewise, there are lines in which I have chosen to retain words or phrases some may find offensive. As an artist, I paint with the colors available to me, compose with the full range of notes on the scale. That said, if any poem with a "bad word" is also a bad poem, that is another matter altogether.

If there is a reader to whom my heart inclined throughout the drafting and revising of these poems it is anyone whose relationship with "religion" is strained or broken and who is familiar with struggle and the hope for something more or better or more real. I am a believer. This does not make struggle or sickness or layoffs or dying go away. At the best moments, I've a lively sense of God's sustaining love for all things and me right there in the mix; at other moments, there is silence, fear, a sense of vast distances, absence, and I cling to faithful words and sacramental acts that speak blindly of what may lie beyond their otherwise empty occurrences. Early in the composition of this sequence, I drafted a line that captured my sense of purpose for the project as a whole: "Every word, a stand against losing heart." I still believe it.

A final paragraph about the volume you hold: it is divided into five sections or "books" following the traditional five-book division of the biblical Psalter. The one-hundred fifty poems in Opening King David are in conversation sequentially with the Bible's one-hundred fifty psalms. As a navigational help, there is, atop the first page of each poem, a quotation or triggering verse from its corresponding psalm.

Acknowledgments

Grateful acknowledgment is made to Emerald City Books—Ian Creeger, in particular—and to the editors of the journals where the following poems or versions of these poems first appeared:

Anglican Theological Review: "At the St. Francis Yacht Club"

Ascent: "Eucharist"

Christianity & Literature: "A Watchman's Song," "*Philia*"

City Works: "Judgment," "The Good Life According to *Architectural Digest*"

Connecticut Review: "Instructions, with a Question," "No Worries," "50," "Genuine Replications"

Image: "Common as Air"

Louisville Review: "Anticipating Our Retirement"

Main Street Rag: "So," "Answer Me," "Crossing the Williamsburg Bridge"

The Other Journal: "Praise Him"

Rock & Sling: "Enter God," "The Centerfielder," "In Heaven"

St Katherine Review: "Off Jake's Pier" (*forthcoming*)

Tar River Poetry: "Neighbor as Theologian," "Waiting"

The following poems appeared in the chapbook *Short List of Wonders*, selected by Dick Allen as winner of the Sunken Garden Poetry Prize and published in 2005 by the Hill-Stead Museum, Farmington, CT: "Ashere," "Instructions, with a Question," "The Wicked Man," "Shortsighted," "No Worries," "*Imitatio*," "Joy," "50," "Two Ways," "The Vulture Tree," "Litany for an Empire," "Less is More," "Sing for Joy," "Better Far," "Glory," "Genuine

Replications," "After a Snowfall," "No Vile Thing," "Insomniac's Commission," "Short List of Wonders," "Good Things"

"Waiting" was reprinted on the Verse Daily website, 11 May 2006.

"Procession" won the 2009 International Arts Movement poetry prize (Bret Lott, judge)

"Praise Him" was included in the book, *"God is Dead" and I Don't Feel So Good Myself* (Cascade Books, 2010)

Finally, I am delighted to acknowledge poet/editor Robert R. McQuilkin, whose small press, Antrim House, published all the poems (or versions of them) in this volume under the four titles *Though War Break Out* (2005), *Song of the Drunkards* (2007), *No Vile Thing* (2008), and *Like Those Who Dream* (2008). His excitement for and blessing of this iteration of the sequence is deeply satisfying.

Book One

Blessed is he who meditates day and night.
Psalm 1:1–2

ASHRE

This time the collision wasn't fatal;
I knocked the doe off the road and backed up

to check. In my low beams, her head high,
those giant black eyes blinked slowly, confused.

Difficult this morning to concentrate
on the psalmic text—*Happy is the man*

whose delight is in the law of the Lord—
which feels irrelevant to everything

that has been flailing at my heart these days.
But how else to learn an answer for how

the tyranny of bleak appearances
drains the soul of all will to persevere?

He is a tree whose leaf does not wither.
I am like chaff that the wind blows away.

HARD TIMES

We wait out this blizzard at the far edge
of whatever suffering it may pile on

the less well kept. Easy for us to love
the bride-white beauty through our air-tight

windows or even brave the elements
one well-plowed mile for two-dollar coffees

at our favorite Zagat-rated café.
Never without a log for the fireplace,

we are thankful for our comforts, though we
sign contracts for these benefits insured

by policies that conspire against all
for whom there remains no room in the inn.

Easy to feel the innkeeper's bind
with the wind chill pushing twenty below.

May your blessing be on your people.
Psalm 3:8

AMONG THE LIVING

We lie down and sleep; and we wake again.
Like dying, or the way I wish it were.

The Lord gives to his beloved sleep, but
few care. Those who do I tend to welcome

as I do your eyes morning to morning.
Evening to evening, the pace picking up,

we lie down and sleep; we wake again,
our field of vision—blink—stroboscopic.

Blink again—we are surrounded by foes
who loathe our sloth, regard my love

to laze beside you of no benefit
to the commonweal. Which is true. So I

may quit my day job. What will they say then?
We lie down and sleep—and wake again.

How long, O men, will you love delusions and seek false Gods?
Psalm 4:2

AGAINST SOLIPSISM

Is it unacceptably romantic
to say aloud that urban poetry

reads as if it needs to get out more, needs
more than a holiday in the country

to curb its solipsistic tendencies?
Most of the universe is—pause—nature.

Imagine hip-hop referring to plums
or an Ashbery knockoff ascending

into the euphony of coherence.
What makes sense of anything that happens

behind locked doors is that which has no need
of a door, real or metaphorical,

to upset one's cognitive apple cart.
Say, the slightest breeze beneath a doorjamb.

Their throat is an open grave.
Psalm 5:9

MOTO AT BROADWAY AND HEWES

Brooklyn, NYC

Whatsoever is vulgar—sub-
standard housing, most packaged goods,

souls lacking virtuous aspiration,
anything ignoble or half-assed—will,

when the splendor appears, be swept up,
collected like so much rubbish, burned.

Imagine earth's spirit clarified,
the good body set free from corruption.

Until then, there is music
for voice and double bass in cafés

where—think temples of refuge—
fugitive hope may find sanctuary.

When the splendor appears, who
will not see it? Whose knee will not bow?

My bones are in agony.
Psalm 6:2

DESIRE

I want to live
      where no one lies
           to the suffering child who asks
How long?

Deceive a child
      and she dies a little—
           a little death, a little death
then gone.

He who is pregnant with evil gives birth to disillusionment.
Psalm 7:14

NARCISSUS POETICUS

unlike the heady air of paperwhites,
my slow, odoriferous return

to dust. We are full of what? *Shit* occurs
to me. And the Spirit would concur.

True, it is said when we pray, our words
are, to God, as incense. But how is this?

For they are rank with resistance
to the holy and with lust, their language

reeking with vengeance toward our enemies.
Deliver us, good Lord, from awful praying.

May the rhetorically repulsive be
removed to an air-tight composter.

Not so my blooming paperwhites. I enter
the apartment, inhale—and remember:

You have set your glory above the heavens.
Psalm 8:1

INSTRUCTIONS, WITH A QUESTION

On a clear dry night, assign the bright stars
proximity, the dim ones the greater

distances; give your sight time to adjust,
and the heavens will assume relative

dimension, seem to deepen.
Tell your high-minded scientific friends

to lighten up, get the picture: Milton's
winged Satan, hungry, descending from sphere

to sphere, eyeing the sparrow-brained and blind.
Humankind, that is. Lunch meat. Look again:

the moon and planets, stars and, it would seem,
nothing else. Good thing, bad thing? Nothing

we can do about it. Any number
of futures left wholly to us. And that glory!

Let the nations know they are but men.
Psalm 9:20

FORGET GOD

"It is natural to fight," he says, leaning
against the water cooler, the counselor's

room tight with boys with suntanned chests.
His name is Jorge. He is from Mexico.

Later that night, he will also tell us
we do not know how to treat a woman.

This is not a movie. It is Tuesday.
We are all sixteen years old and looking

for a truth to try on like a boxer's robe.
(What is summer camp good for, if not this?)

Jorge's truth is pure silk—"Hermanos,
nature compels our defense of high ground"—

and we believe everything he says,
beginning, that night, with his eyes and grin.

His enemies are crushed, they collapse.
Psalm 10:10

THE WICKED MAN

Opening King David, the reader may
resist initially the heavy ink

against "the wicked man," dismiss the pitch
as rhetorically transparent, the cant

of every royal house, their fear showing.
This reader may also own a horse farm,

manage a hedge fund. Other readers—
think poor and disenfranchised, the wards

of insolvent nation-states—are without
hope in this heavy world, except one: God

will break the arms of all who hold themselves
beyond account. The wicked man

is no mere figure of speech.
Ask the miserable.

When the foundations are being destroyed,
what can the righteous do?
Psalm 11:3

SNAPSHOT

Psalm Eleven, here's the picture: of a god
who hates all purveyors of violence

and answers their mere bows and arrows with
an apocalyptic maelstrom. What I see:

a comedy—no laughing matter—where
the villains receive what they've intended

for their victims, who then inherit all
the thugs had planned for themselves. Think Esther.

But who gives a damn for any of this
or cares what it may mean? See there, outside

the window, the faithfulness of daybreak
slanting orange through a scrim of new snow.

We own our lips—who is our master?
Psalm 12:4

REASONS I WRITE

Those who assume they have no one
to whom they must account for their words—

like politicians, bankers, older brothers,
theologians, poets, headmasters—

they are wrong. *Every knee will bow, every
tongue confess.* So I do not use words

like "shit" or "Sovereign Lord" unaware.
Berryman, after Hopkins, wrote truly:

that line about Christ being the only
just critic. I write because it takes little

to spark my rage, and Saint Paul said we must
toil with our hands for the end of anger

is murder, and if any would be saved,
they must, *with fear and trembling,* work it out.

I will sing to the Lord, for he has been good to me.
Psalm 13:6

AMONG LUMINOUS THINGS

In this ocean of ordinary light,
we are reef dwellers. Whether brain coral

or parrot fish or moray, we all do
our bit, then die. The ocean teems entire,

a whole we believe by faith, wrestling
with the darkness and sorrow in our hearts.

I will never regard as wise the fool
who would have me slap a muzzle on

the voice within, small and still, inspiring
praise of whoever it may be who holds

all this in brilliant fullness. I say
let fly with adoration, thanks, and more,

for if this is not the deeper reason
we are here, then there is no reason.

God is present.
Psalm 14:5

SHORTSIGHTED

for Bill, believer and photographer

You shoot the glorious—a crimson leaf
clinging to a bare branch, a snow-gray sky—

yet hanker for glory, that pure essence
of the uncreated Father of lights.

Though not one to say there is no God,
I am stuck on the quip about the bird

in hand being better than any two
that may be futzing about in the bush.

No doubt heaven's great, but this here's amazing.
Go ahead, call me shortsighted. It's true:

I'm happy camping in light's gallery
and praising the hard, full-spectrum effects

of here—now—ahead of me, a red fox
on the pond trail taking her own sweet time.

Lord, who may dwell in your sanctuary?
Psalm 15:1

EUCHARIST

Never have I felt a natural draw
to work anywhere close to an altar,

though, with this loose pile of sticks laid neatly
on a bare patch of earth, the ambition

to live quietly, minding my business,
becomes oblation, an ordinary

work of hands in service to grace. No priest
required, no victim, knife, or temple tax.

To this ground may a sweet, heavenly fire
descend. Here, where air sickens with the stench

of war and the perfunctory smoke
of religious ceremony, I turn—

keep us safe, O Lord our God—
to collect windfall for the coming night.

The sorrows of those will increase who run after other gods.
Psalm 16:4

RUSH HOUR

I saw troops patrolling Grand Central,
teams of police boarding trains to

and from the universe. In the name of
Code Orange we station gun-bearers

wherever, whenever we feel exposed.
On the train ride out, I draw attention

to a piece of luggage by itself.
The porter assured me the owner

asked to put it there, but I worry
the foreign-born porter was lying.

Is no one, nowhere safe? Hours later
turning onto campus, I wave to Sarge

in his pickup keeping watch by night.
Not even the faithful. . .

As for the deeds of men—
Psalm 17:4

SHE SAID

Let the Spirit write the poems through you.
Yet the Spirit I know works in us as we

work on things like love—putting out the trash
without having to be reminded—which

I am very far from getting right. Poems
may serve love, but it would not be God's way

to bypass our humanity to make
texts pleasing to him. Otherwise they might

emerge in meadows like rocks urged up through
topsoil by freeze and thaw. To hell with poems.

What matters: some help with love, for we who
frame laws and build flimsy arguments

resist at every turn the Spirit's work
and shut our hearts against the gentle friend.

He brought me out into a spacious place.
Psalm 18:19

SETH'S POND, WEST TISBURY

All things hold together.
Colossians 1:17

Two lady's-slippers up along the path,
a kingfisher, the indifferent moon

still hanging in a brilliant, mid-spring sky,
my son in a sweater in a rowboat—

thank you. I choose to believe
the universe not merely big, but chock-full

with presence. Yet may the pessimist be
right about us—pitiable flecks of dust?

With terror in the air, the NBA
shifting into All-Star mode, and ninety

e-mails to clear by Monday, what is true?
(Why, O my soul, do you prattle on thus?)

A tall reed gives slightly in the cool breeze,
nearly buckles when a redwing alights.

Their voice goes out into all the earth.
Psalm 19:4

SO

If all created things speak wordlessly
of their creator—a turkey's wattle?—

then what do tax loopholes say about us?
Or bombed-out cities? The gossip of blue

highways—quaint, inaudible buzz—is it
praise or lamentation? Could even these

restless streams make glad the heart of God?
Old Madeline *(Wind in the Door)* L'Engle

says all true art, looking death in the face
and rising into light, feeds "the River."

O, to be able to hear, unfiltered,
the riotous vertical tongues of trees

and see beneath their cowled humility
the fire that burns yet will not consume them.

May the Lord send help from Zion.
Psalm 20:1–2

ANSWER ME

Bill's a friend, homeowner, married man—says
their small lakeside place has begun to feel

too much for them—can't seem to keep up with
what's breaking down—and back on campus

"well done" has become a moving target
he quit trying to hit months ago. No

surprise his wish to remain here has quit
on him—Donna starts round eight of chemo

next week. This morning my wife surprised me:
"If Bill decides to leave, we should leave, too."

What's left to keep us staying anywhere
when, despite faith, hope, love, we keep losing

ground to discouragement, the suspicion
that no amount of work will ever be enough?

Root out their seed from among the children of men.
Psalm 21:10

SHOCK AND AWE

Little words build, become fighting words,
and before you know it, some enemy

has us believing our cause is righteous.
Which is when our poets, like prophets

or sorely agitated roosters, take
courage and launch preemptory psalms,

smart bombs aimed at the heads of the wicked.
Pretty ugly stuff.
               Today, as I prayed

in a local wildlife sanctuary,
two kestrels rose from the meadow, hovered

like the Spirit above the primal sea,
and clarified my way forward. Holding

to beauty, I must leave the rest to others
who may not hear the word of April wings.

I am a worm and not a man.
Psalm 22:6

IN FACT

Show me an absolutely placid mind,
and I'll show you a corpse or one as good

as dead: one in denial of the swill—
the lies of desire—I keep falling for.

Try as we may, we cannot lift ourselves
from ourselves rabbit-from-hat-like and live

to tell of it, though liars make bundles
claiming otherwise. We are a mess, yet

it pleases Him—and let us quit whining
about the gender of divinity—

to be numbered among the conflicted.
So here, among yappy dogs, snorting bulls,

bone-thin cows, let us offer God our praise:
Damn, you're beautiful; and your handiwork.

The Lord is my shepherd.
Psalm 23:1

23

Roger loathes being likened to a sheep,
struggles with self-esteem, takes the figure

as an affront to his intelligence.
Arlys loves Roger, so when the preacher

went on for twenty minutes about sheep,
the Shepherd, and the sheep pen, Arlys winced

and prayed for Roger. Prayed he would not want
to walk home alone, cancel their outing

to the state park, return to the city.
Arlys loves God, believes Roger's doubting

could be turned to confidence overnight.
If only he would hear the Shepherd's voice,

she would sleep beside him in the fold, lack
nothing, anoint his head with oil.

CROSSING THE WILLIAMSBURG BRIDGE

Easter morning

Walt Whitman's Brooklyn behind us, we are walking
to Manhattan and a late brunch in Chinatown:

steamed dumplings, rooster sauce, pan-fried sesame bread,
plastic bowls of spicy mushroom soup, oolong tea.

We walk above traffic, the river; beside the JMZ line,
share elevated pedestrian lanes with cyclists, Hassidim,

speed walkers, hippies, Latinos, arty types in all black.
You are here—a mantra learned from maps on kiosks

in suburban malls—plays in my head, and softly (to myself)
I offer up an Easter hymn under Jerusalem-blue skies.

All families will bow before him; he is the King of glory.
To the south, a thin column of cloud rises like altar smoke.

The earth is the Lord's, and the fullness thereof.
In this light, even the jaded skyline stands transfigured.

He instructs sinners in his ways.
Psalm 25:8

WITH BILL AT BAFFLIN SANCTUARY

We walk woodland trails cut by volunteers
and kid about total depravity

which, pertaining to salvation, translates
even "the greatest geniuses are blind-

er than moles." The path is soft underfoot,
the laurel late-blooming. Beside a pond

he unpacks his camera. Can a snapshot
reveal the affliction of our nature?

I take refuge under translucent leaves,
leave him to his patient compositions.

But what's the point? His kind wife is dying,
and he has left the house to take pictures

of ferns uncurling. Do I hear myself?
Are they not—forgive me—portraits of her?

Test me, O Lord, and try me.
Psalm 26:2

GENERAL CONFESSION

In each promise of faithfulness, traces
of countless betrayals: averted eyes,

a voice's tremor. Like the air we breathe
or the glances we exchange with strangers

on strobe-lit dance floors, we test positive
for impurity. But do not expect

a list of lurid details in these lines;
I am neither Catholic nor Lowell nor Plath.

I am merely—how does the song go—"prone
to wander." So have we any chance,

this side of heaven, at a constant heart?
Or even modest progress toward that end?

The word's out: *love covers a multitude
of sins.* Is this the best we can hope for?

I will see the goodness of the Lord in the land of the living.
Psalm 27:13

TO SELF-PITY

What a force you are! Cyclonic, godlike,
irresistible as lust is irresistible, and thick

with generations of flung wreckage, blunt
as thugs. Who, coracled in mere feeling,

can stand against such compelling torque?
I confess: you are a familiar ride, a drug

of choice, a sluttish changeling, your blouse
half-unbuttoned, eyes fierce with loathing.

Where, in my soul's fluid world, currents
meet, there, turning on the slightest axis

of an insecurity, you—siren vortex—
draw me into your sweet, insatiable self.

Old friend and nemesis, there, too, a Rock
of refuge may be found. To Him I cleave.

Be their shepherd and carry them forever.
Psalm 28:9

NO WORRIES

for my tour guide at the interview

We take them as they come, ages twelve
to nineteen, dress them in blue blazers, and run

them ragged. We get away with it because
their parents worry, and the lawns are presidential.

If we do one thing well it is attending
to the millions of surfaces that present themselves

to a visitor's eye at each turn along
the arcing, neatly bordered pathways. All this

beneath broad, heavy-leafed trees not native
to this corner of the state: copper beech,

ginkgo, weeping red maple. We are a world apart,
not entirely to ourselves, just safely to one side.

But it was not the brick dorms or landscaping,
the dress code or college list that drew me

twenty years ago to these lawns, this life decked
with adolescents. It was the canvas hammock

you said most visitors never see slung across
the stream—between two birches—behind the rink.

Fall and spring, you and your friends would go there
and one at a time climb into the heavy cotton, pull

the frayed sides up across your chests and swing,
companions pumping the ropes for you, and all the way

to the top you'd turn, face nothing but the water
beneath you, then over you'd go—again

and again—wrapped in the weathered chrysalis.
I cannot say exactly what it was about that

late April afternoon that won me over to the job,
but I will be ever grateful for the detour.

The God of glory thunders.
Psalm 29:3

NEIGHBOR AS THEOLOGIAN

How can she talk about a "word from God"?
The weather, yes, or the fate of our hedge.

A snake or the shrinking odds of her spouse
beating cancer, sure. But a word from God?

As though God were an actual person,
albeit incomprehensibly vast.

Yet this is how she talks, the way I talk
about my son from whom I could never

hear too much or too often, who's only
hours away in Brooklyn. Why, unless

my sin were envy, would I begrudge her
an assurance of contact? More likely,

I long for what she has, embarrassed, pained
by my lack of openness to mystery—

which, she has told me, is wholly present
in, with, and under the hedge between us.

When you hid your face, I was dismayed.
Psalm 30:7

AS IT IS

The face of God is hidden from me.
I see only old walls, the clutter

of familiar rooms, shelves of books, snapshots,
mix-and-match decor. Awake or asleep

and dreaming, no divine shook-foil glimmer
for my inmost eye. Rumors reach me

of others' encounters—glimpses of His face—
but after devouring these, the want

remains. Is there some special training I need?
Last week a friend confided that for years

the Holy Ghost has shimmered inside her,
every moment beatific. My resolve:

to pretend my friend is not a liar
or schizophrenic—and to seek new friends.

He showed his wonderful love to me when I was in a besieged city.
Psalm 31:21

PUTTING A NAME TO THE FACE

In Madagascar or Peru, St. Kitts
or Tasmania, wherever children,

despite suffering, find games to play
or halt play to marvel at a column

of clouds collecting on some horizon;
wherever anyone takes care to make

ready a back room for a visitor—
sweep the floor for the ten-thousandth time,

place a fresh flower on the pillow—there
a glimpse, the face you know you know

in a crowd of strangers who disappears
before you get a fix on the distance

between you—
            mercy!—
                        and that face.

Do not be like the horse or the mule which have no understanding.
Psalm 32:9

BROTHER CHRONOS

Radio-controlled and programmed to check
in every four hours with an atomic

device deep in some bunker in Denver,
my travel clock is more monk than truant

on probation, for it desires correction,
six times a day turns out toward the big

unseen—receives it—then turns back
to serving my fascination with time.

No trumpet sounds to signal the clock's
connecting moment—a mute faithfulness

wholly independent of audience—
and I would be its disciple, pray the hours,

live contented, in step with the Spirit,
but my program is a prison named fear.

Still, how wonderful to know what time it is,
precise to within a millionth of a second.

From heaven the Lord looks down and sees all mankind.
Psalm 33:13

REPORT

I flavor my food with long suffering.

The clothes in my closet are unironed.

I have never spoken in another tongue.

Given the option, I would work alone

or in the tested company of friends.

I find nothing holy in national

holidays though love getting the hours

off, time being the skin I look forward

to shedding once I am done with my life.

Between Eden and the New Earth, only

wind, music, and diligence feel at all

familiar. Here, everywhere is exile.

I will continue to speak this language.

Every word, a stand against losing heart.

No one will be condemned who takes refuge in him.
Psalm 34:22

GOD

Are all theophobic? No one wants to
be reminded. No thought, sentence, or deed

can escape the chill of divine review.
Dread being a dark matter of the soul,

engines of suppression hum constantly
flooding the wakeful mind with distractions

grand as virtue, common as relatives.
(How else to prevent the unwanted Word's

indelicate meaning from causing hurt?)
Judgment by one's peers can be useful, but

keep at bay the cool scrutiny of God
lest "luv" lose its warm inclusivity,

"my truth" its fragile singularity.
No "truth," though lovely, will be left standing

on the day Truth absolutely arrives.
Poor, middle class, rich; straight, gay—no one

questions the myth: autonomy, each one's
rule a law. But those who *fear the Lord* and

seek Him *lack nothing*, their fear a spring-fed
tributary to perfect freedom where

unruly wills find rest in serving Him.
Voice-beyond-language (still, small, holy),

wickedness reveals itself resisting
(xenophobically) Thy sovereign wisdom.

Yesterday, today, tomorrow, folly's
zero swallows her dreary children whole.

I will give thanks in the great assembly.
Psalm 35:18

WORD PROBLEM

They sit facing him in three rows, each row elevated six inches above the one in front of it, and on each tier, three narrow curved tables. In the first row sit four conferees per table, in the second five, and the third six. Looking at them from the lectern, he counts forty-five in all—not one familiar or getting any younger—though if he hadn't known in advance, he'd have never guessed it was a roomful of fifty-one year olds. He makes forty-six, and as he looks at them, he calmly studies his response to every different tie, chin, nose, hairline, as if sitting before him were as many versions of himself as populate his unconscious and this were a summit of his selves. The topic: a spiritual cost/benefit analysis of the respective merits of reading, aerobic exercise, and contributing to the commonweal, with narrative implications for both the good life and dying well. Why else would forty-five busy fifty-one year olds agree to gather in this three-tiered conference room? Why else would he be addressing them?

The evildoers lie fallen—thrown down, not able to rise.
Psalm 36:12

TWO WORLDS

1.

From multinational corporations
to international regulatory agencies,

from rogue states and terror cells
to the holy democratic empire—

behind it all, a clever, loose alliance
of "powers and principalities" fueling

fires more terrible than Mordor's.
Has anyone an oracle against this world?

By what spirit would the sayer speak?
Would he wrap himself in vestments

and deliver prophecies like a saint?
Or strap on a hissing Telecaster,

step to the microphone, and rip the tops
off the heads of all who fear nothing

but their own loss of say in how
the business of this world gets done.

2.

There is another world—where Orion,
like an older brother, drops by each year

on my October birthday, and the glory
of the cosmos is all signal, no noise.

Here the mountains we walk among rise
from pristine fiords, each silver river

a sacrament by which we and all things
thrive side by side; day or night

no clever snake or shadow deceives. Here
the prayers of all those waylaid

by the other world and left for dead
have found their audience; faith knows

what may not be confirmed. So it is
two worlds inhere. The one I love: a vast,

endless miracle in super-slow-mo
extending through and beyond Nike.

Consider the blameless.
Psalm 37:37

IN MINISTRY

We dress for the job, learn to speak right,
when required, employ polysyllabics.

Yet what's to keep us from being found out?
We are a field of splendid grasses

soon to vanish like smoke from a ruin.
How we strive to gain the dominical inch

we know will guarantee a reputation!
How, indeed, to be revered by generations!

And I am straining in that same field
for that same reward. O Lord, have mercy.

I have become like a man whose mouth can offer no reply.
Psalm 38:14

ON SILENCE, BRIEFLY

for Barry Moser, artist and teacher

Fifteen, winter term,

we arrive early, no noise
but him breathing through his beard,

his pen's thin metal quill skating across the rough ice
of handmade rag paper,

a broad-lipped lady's-slipper emerging.

You are the one who has done this.
Psalm 39:9

LORD

Get off my back. For a season
obsess over another's
imperfection.
With you constantly
reviewing my little existence,
what shot have I at joy?
Your beauty
amplifies my homeliness.
How I long to sing before I die,
but as your project
I have become a mute
phantom pacing.
Is it so wicked to want a little
rest for my soul? Behold
what your scrutiny
works in me: heaviness of heart,
ceaseless introspection;
with your eye upon me—
noble moth
that I amount to—all hope
has flown. What are
a man's chances against the prince
of righteousness? Please,
take a break. Book
a holiday cruise to elsewhere.
At the very least,

listen to my cry, O God:
Look away from me,
that I may rejoice again
before I depart and am no more.

Happy the man who does not trust in such as go about with lies.
Psalm 40:4

CROSSING THE NOTCH

for Deb

In tight, fast-wicking garb and hiking boots,
he looked like someone who would know

how much farther we had
to where the Long Trail met the notch road,

so when he told us we were nowhere near
and would need to retrace our slow

steps back up and across the icy ridge,
our sweat-soaked cotton clothes grew heavier.

Knees failing us, even the light breeze
of a late-October mid-afternoon became

an enemy plotting our ruin, and in that
trail-side exchange, our hike

revealed itself as pure folly, potentially dire.
Who, O Lord, is not a novice, an amateur

in this business of setting out and arriving?
So progress came down to a bushwhacker's

word versus the confidence of us flatlanders
in a cryptic text on a trailhead sign

and occasional glimpses of thin white blazes.
Finally, we pushed past him

and, inside a descending hour, found
ourselves—despite the grand indifference

of a shadowless day in northern Vermont—
safely on the narrow road through the notch.

Blessed is he who has regard for the weak.
Psalm 41:1

AMEN & AMEN

When Cory told me how a friend's daughter,
from the fifth floor of a hotel along the route,

sent the entire dark-suited security phalanx
of a presidential motorcade into a mad scramble

by her unladylike middle finger raised in protest,
I wondered where I was, what year, what country.

Then I read an interview with a retired general
speculating that the detonation of a WMD

on these shores would spark a wholesale scrapping
of both the Constitution and Bill of Rights,

and thirty difficult years of putting history behind me
dissolved, the scene changed, the woods out back

suddenly defoliated, a rank odor fouling the air.
How long had I been asleep? I am stunned

with the burden of my countless accommodations
to denial. Show mercy, O Christ, and preserve

my heart's freedom to see and honor the beauty
of your hand in all things good, right, and true.

Renew the faith of that angry daughter.
Even as shadows lengthen inevitably toward

the darkness when no one can work, strengthen
my knees that I may not falter along the way

that leads through the valley of terror.
In this present—wherever we are, whatever

year it may be—raise up an unconquerable chorus
of resistance and praise, from everlasting to everlasting.

Book Two

These things I remember.
Psalm 42:4

IMITATIO

"Ah, this! New snow to my knees. The warming reach
of early morning sunlight. The air hung with fullness. . . ."

What she read to us from her journal a week before
she had two liters drained from her cancerous lungs.

Every Thursday after supper, she and Bill drop by
to join the small circle of friends who gather to pray

and listen for God's voice in the stillness of Scripture.
Sometimes we sing. Sometimes we share what we

call God sightings. Sometimes we laugh so hard
one or more of us stumble from the room wheezing.

Bill has taken a leave of absence from work to care
for Donna. Ah, this: loss of stamina, shortness of breath—

as a deer pants for streams of water, that sort of thing.
After prayer, Donna spoke of a satisfaction deeper

than what follows a slow walk in the woods, a month
of good reports, or a quiet evening losing track

of whatever time it may take for a long bath, longer
massage, pillow talk beyond a doctor's recommendation.

That Thursday, Bill sat with her on the couch, eyes closed.
They deny themselves no good thing, not even praise.

Send forth your light and guide me to the place where you dwell.
Psalm 43:3

IN THE NEW YEAR

Times Square, Manhattan: one million souls
assemble, then disperse, and though not

everyone's retelling of the event will be
disappointment-free, the larger story

of so many coming in and going out smacks
of a general restraint so glorious one might

see God all over it. Yet that weekend
who makes the front page of the Sunday Times

but a mouthy teen from Toledo who refused
to slip the assistant principal's bowling shirt

over her navel-baring violation of the school code.
Musterion tes anomias: all hell breaking loose

in Ohio, of all places. The girl is fourteen—
handcuffed, booked, detained in a holding cell—

and whether she passes ninth grade or not,
her little story won out over the big

story of how tens of thousands of teens
in the Midwest managed that day to dress okay,

navigate a schedule of major and minor
scholastic commitments, plus gym, and thus

defer busloads of instant gratification
in exchange for making slow, quiet gains

on any number of American dreams.
According to Times correspondent Sara Rimer,

the girl said the bowling shirt was "real ugly."

You no longer go out with our armies.
Psalm 44:9

ROOFING THE BALLS

Quickly at the end of recess, kickball
having been summarily concluded
by the scowl of a bell, we would grab
the red rubber gym balls and, from the base
of the playground's two-story north wall,
punt them onto the flat roof of the schoolhouse
and hightail it to our classrooms.

Of course we knew better, but
we were so tough,
the stuff of future varsities
and gunboat patrols on the Mekong Delta.
We owned those balls the way we owned
our reputations, so if we
couldn't play with them, no one would.

Four slow decades on,
I am still at school, but now my work
is to unlearn that original arrogance—fluffed
by championship rings, purple
hearts, advanced degrees—and become
the very kind—think overalls, broom closet—
for whom, back then, we toughs
had no regard: the kind
our parents' taxes paid to have climb
the dark stairwell to the schoolhouse roof,
gather up those errant balls, and, for the next
round of children at recess, throw them back down.

SILLY SALLY

One rule: tell no one the rules.

Permissive democracies, like Silly Sally, love
queers, hate fundamentalism. So we invent
new, improved social formulae presuming
to possess critical insight and freedom to do so.
Silly Sally loves freedom, hates rules; loves
marriage, hates traditional definitions. If
all are equal and any want to be wed, then

each is entitled to it. Or something like that.
Silly Sally loves syllogisms, hates hearing "no."
Once kings hired poets to memorialize war,
pen royal epithalamia, and otherwise raise
ebenezers to the king's glory in the king's tongue.
Silly Sally loves babble, hates word games.
Now our democracies rely on the university

to do the king's work, the king being
less flesh-'n-blood personal, more ideological,
more high prince of the powers of the air, less
a single, identifiable monarch. Silly Sally
loves butterflies, hates carpenter ants. Today
may be the past we regret tomorrow—I hear
the slurge of a washing machine on rinse cycle—

though this presumes a capacity for regret
will remain operative when the new, so-called
morality has released us from old inhibitions.

Silly Sally loves permissiveness, hates detergent
with bleach; loves green, hates democracy.
Lately, the writers I have preferred reading
squeeze out their lines after work, between loads.

He lifts his voice, the earth melts.
Psalm 46:6

UNDER THE SUN

On these leveled acres of lawn
surrounded by stately brick dorms, slate
roofs rippling in an April heat wave,

students lie out like soldiers in a field
or laundry on riverside rocks
ready for folding or for burial.

Last week, we buried a young alum.
"The kid the rest of us wanted to be,"
a dry-eyed classmate said

and grabbed my arm, the sudden
protest of her tears no respecter of age
or station in life or the politics

of grief, that old impassivity
like a hard, waterless moon pacing
round and round a cold, blue-boned body.

God is seated on his holy throne.
Psalm 47:8

JOY

Topic of the sermon in that store front church in Detroit.
A new believer, I was miserable, my faith still in the grip
of what had nearly destroyed me: outrage at the pointless
war, assassinations, riots, the absurdity of country club
conversations. The preacher did not wear robes.
The Lord's Table was a folding affair unadorned
by embroidered linens and towering brass candlesticks.
He did not raise his voice theatrically. Joy, he said to us, is
serious business, less an emotion, more a destination. Think
of Jesus, his agony; scripture says he endured the Cross,
the shame and pain of it, for the joy set before him—
like a splendid banquet in a dream about a wedding.
The congregation did not kneel to pray or rise to proceed
to an altar rail to receive the bread and wine. That evening
Christ came to us on small trays, in plastic cups, and we all
ate and drank together. I do not remember the music,
but I'm sure we sang. I'm sure some among us lifted hands
to Him who made of our bumbling praise a momentary throne.
At the end of the service, as I exited quietly,
a big man in a white tee shirt put his hand on my shoulder,
introduced himself, said he drove trucks for a living
and that he had felt the Lord bidding him to speak.
Not knowing anything about me, he told me that if
I seek the Dove, it will fly away, but if I seek the Lord,
the Dove will come. He did not lead me in a prayer
or ask my name. Before I had time to thank him, he was off

who-knows-where, and I was left to look for my ride,
the married friends to whose home I hitchhiked that week.
This was their church. The preacher their friend.
And although I believe that what he said about joy is true,
I still pray for a visitation, the flutter of ecstasy, release,
the heavy world as much an encumbrance as it ever was.

. . . in the city of our God.
Psalm 48:8

WAITING

With no enduring city here, no
homestead or ancestral cemetery
to ground a sense of belonging,

what reaches in to shape a vision
is beauty. Hey, it's everywhere:
not only in lakes and flower gardens,

but peeking over a Kmart facade
and slanting off parking lot puddles.
Compositions abound, planned

or haphazard, that leak the news:
*yes, here, too, beauty tabernacles
among us*—the way an abandoned

shopping cart points to the white
Salvation Army donation bin
and, beyond, toward a stand of trees

hung with crows that crowds
the lot's perimeter. Salvation. Now
there's a beautiful rumor: that I may

trade-in my load of moral pain, my fear
of being found out and shamed,
and right away recover a bit of what

I most want to see more of:
the beauty of holiness.
                              Here,

stationed solo on the paved crown
of this hill, parked and waiting
for my family, I follow the crows'

jerky line of flight as they rise up
from their rain-darkened perches
and set out for nowhere in particular.

With the harp I will expound my riddle.
Psalm 49:4

NO COMFORT HERE

Between those who trust in their wealth
and those who trust in the sayings
of those who trust in their wealth, synergy

like miles of thick rope—enough to hang
each of them til ravenous death
hath glutted itself on their patrimony.

These are words they who are of this world
cannot hear yet must listen to, the way
bulls must listen to their butchers'

coarse joking. But this is not a joke,
and whosoever fails to grieve their sentence
numbers himself among the non-hearing.

Can this be said more plainly?

There is no comfort in safety, only
safety and an ancient rumor of promises
for which there are no guarantees. So

as the beasts will die, the rich will die—
in their fabulous mansions on lands named
after themselves—without understanding.

Do I eat the flesh of bulls or drink the blood of goats?
Psalm 50:13

50

The category, bad assumptions. Chief
among them: that the I AM is

like us or any one of us—needy,
vengeful, petty—and that what we think

is true of God, from history or nature
or holy writ, will stand when he appears

and we behold the beauty unmediated.
A personal note: I draw my assumptions

of God from my read of what is
evident in the gospels' take on Jesus.

So I may contradict myself, but
it is the best I know to do this side

of believing that the word "God" points
to one who truly is God and well

beyond all proximate images we may
forge that would satisfy our need

to shrink all things to what we
can grasp and pass on to our children.

The irony: that unless our proximate images
dissolve in our children's mouths

and open them to the irreducible mystery,
they will choke on them and perish.

Not a happy picture: we parents placing
razor blades on our children's' tongues.

You desire truth in the inner parts.
Psalm 51:6

AT HER EIGHTIETH BIRTHDAY PARTY

Aunt El says YHWH
is a poor god with nothing
to offer but himself,

and if that's not enough,
then we are free
to invest our sad

hearts elsewhere. I am
fifty-one and obeying
what Jesus said

about making friends
with unrighteous mammon.
(What other kind is there?)

When I tell her this,
she says I've much to learn
and so much to lose.

IN NEED OF AN EXIT STRATEGY

Though the school looks splendid—
red brick, gray slate, acres of hybrid lawn—

a worm eats at the mortar that binds us
to the good our slow, common work intends.

Surfaces may seem perfectible, but
the soul of a thing? Even a moment's near

perfection is illusive. Easier to trick
a visiting family's eye than earn such trust

as rests on confidence in quality throughout
the process of a thing becoming lovely.

Heavier and less mobile than when
I arrived twenty years ago—who can compete

with the celebrated masters of sheen?—
how much longer will I be welcome here?

By which bloated part will I manage to seal
my doom? "O you deceitful tongue!"

"Insatiable maw." "Stupid prick." Certainly
these cover a fair stretch of the domain

traditionally tagged as condemnable. Yet
another—"stiff neck"—may undo me: unable

to acknowledge any other point of view
as the equal of my all-sufficient own.

God looks down from heaven.
Psalm 53:2

JUDGMENT

Bones are good. Any fool knows
      it's bad to be drawn, bone from bone,
          and quartered.

Scatter the bones of fools,
      and you spoil their best chance
          at finding rest.

Some fools, appealing to God,
      strap explosives to their skin,
          make shrapnel of their bones.

Still, the good of bones abides.
      Even in clever fools
          who know to dress up

their corruption in charity,
      each of their bones is good
          as the moon is good, or old growth,

or the vulture I saw—hollow
      boned—a hundred feet above
          the doughnut shop in Dayville.

Strangers are attacking me. . . ; in your faithfulness
destroy them , O Lord.
Psalm 54:3,5

READING THE PSALTER

My problem: the casual presumption
of psalmists, weaned on miracle stories,

thinking God happy to do their dirty work.
Wouldn't it be nice—*Vengeance is mine,*

says the Lord, I will repay—to be so sure,
as I pass from classroom to squash court

to committee meeting, that I am so—
is *beloved* the right modifier?—so secure

in the knowledge of my preferred status
before the Almighty that I need only

say the word—that colleague's name, those
mockers—and God will carry out the hit. No

trail of evidence. My nervous resolution:
to read aloud no longer the Psalter's

darker lines, in case such audible readings
conspire, *breathe along with* the gross

assumption of God's instant availability
for settling this or that tribal score.

We must—I must do my own dirty work
or else forever hold my difficult peace.

Oh, that I had the wings of a dove! I would fly away and be at rest.
Psalm 55:6

THE COMMUTER

She has been daydreaming of hearing the precise
pulse of dove wings in stereo, head centered

evenly between wing left and wing right,
her attention divided by a shifting landscape

and the constant threat of talons from above. Risk
is unavoidable; she does not have to invent

clever predators in the economic food chain
or her own vulnerability to what would hasten to un-

do her and the quiet life she has labored to insure.
More and more she daydreams of flying over, well

beyond her suburban half-acre into the mountains
drawn by a rumor of large, open rhythms, unaffected

surfaces of immaculate detail, the absence of taxes.
Wilderness serves a different god than she does.

There, all things inhere. Or seem to. Here,
packed into a gently swaying commuter train,

even opposites repel, each seeking its own shelter
from what, like an avenging angel, travels with them.

Record my lament; list my tears on your scroll.
Psalm 56:8

TWO WAYS

Bill says of nature—wave, nebula, birch,
       bufflehead—that it's all
the fractal hem of God's outer garment.

Visiting a friend on the Jersey shore,
       I pointed to a cloud formation:
repeating undulations on the heavens' underbelly.

Not knowing Bill, my host growled,
       "It's a fucking cloud,"
brushed by me, and sank into her house like a stain.

Living anywhere, shit has a way
       of darkening vision, the heart
bearing only so much heaviness before it hardens.

All is suffering, the Buddha said. I wonder:
       if I had only reached forth
a hand to comfort my friend's bitter heart,

would we both have been healed?

I am in the midst of lions.
Psalm 57:4

ON THE BALCONY OF THE RACQUET
& TENNIS CLUB

Between potted plants—the pots hewn from blocks
of granite the size of small cars, the plants
Babylonian—he considers how to bend
light around himself, become
nothing or, if not nothing,
then nothing more than
a mid-air peripheral shimmer
in their visual field who hobnob
at this Park Avenue landmark; he imagines
becoming something spectral, nothing
actually to pursue as he was obliged to pursue
the invitation his boss pressed upon him
to enjoy this mid-week, mid-town bash
at the racquet club and these petite
crab cakes, broad tables of champagne,
skewered scallops. Being overwhelmed by
even the loveliest of phenomena
is not the same as being filled with goods things—
Mary's *agathon*—without which even the wealthiest
roll home *kenous*—empty-handed—
behind their snappy, black-capped chauffeurs.
He knows her Magnificat by heart.
Knows, too, that these in their heels
and silk ties—MBAs and Doctorates
of Jurisprudence—these, too—their memberships

like inviolate kinship bonds—mask
with smooth, articulate elegance
lives common as rice and beans.
Here on the thin margin of this
open-air balcony, between tall, leafy exotics,
he thinks slowly to himself that he has forgotten
so much of his life, and those here
cannot help him remember it.
But he does not care that they cannot. He cares only
that in the morning he will wake up
beside his wife, and they will make a day
for themselves that they will likely
not remember ten or five or, hell, one year
from now. He is not sure anymore
that he even wants to remember his life,
for it would take too many interviews
with too many strangers who would swear
it had been with him that this
or that vivid memory of theirs was made, and how
could he refute it? For now
he wants only to bend the porch
light, city light, star and moonlight, all light
around himself and make good,
from this loveliest of clubs, an unseen exit.

Before your pots can feel the heat of the thorns—whether they be green or dry—the wicked will be swept away.
Psalm 58:9

THE WAY IT IS

For good or ill, I am among the fortunate, the happy
and living on a five-hundred acre estate
kept by a crew I neither have to pay nor oversee.
I have never, involuntarily, gone hungry
or had to pawn rags to shelter my family. Never
have I been pushed to the point of longing
to bathe my feet in the blood of the wicked, who
by force impose their visionary will upon the world.
What I think I know is that everything happens all at once—
privation, birthing stars, regime changes—
and some of it is not good, and how much is not good
is relative to the calculator's point of view.
Certainly what appears to be true is how
what is not good never fails to inspire dangerous humor,
sweet dreams among co-conspirators, bitter lyrics
in beautiful songs—the kind of songs I like best—
deeply felt and aimed at making sensible
to a numbed, happy public—folk like me—the urgencies
of the discontented. And it is true, or I am
sufficiently educated to know how to say it, that
despite my happiness, I, too, cannot wait for the day
when earth steps free of her long bondage to decay
and I find myself, as though I were just
waking up, in a new body equipped with stable knees,
an unencumbered will, and desire like wisdom from above.

O my Strength, I watch for you.
Psalm 59:9

APRIL AGAIN

Too obvious, I say, that black-
bibbed he-sparrow's hots for the she
he races after, making a speedway

of the broad, budding forsythia
not ten feet from the back porch
where I take my morning coffee.

It has been a long winter. And
minus his exuberance, I, too,
am starting these days optimistic

that spring will stick around a while,
all warring factions everywhere
will cease their interminable idiocy

(don't get me started), and seven
prodigious months from now
even the Cubs will own big rings.

Better optimism after waking up
than melancholy. Soon enough—
by noon or certainly come evening—

discouragement will return like
so many snarling dogs prowling
the dark-alley sprawl that crams

my little cranium. So these bright
minutes on the back porch pulling
for the he-sparrow are delicious.

You might say they are daily bread,
crumbs from a table set deep within
a kingdom better than optimism.

Who will bring me to the fortified city?
Psalm 60:9

WHAT I KNOW ABOUT A NEIGHBOR

That he attends faithfully a church
where every Sunday during the main service
a worship leader pilots the congregation
through opening praise songs, a solemn call
to present soul and body to God, then
silence, a corporate confession, and
"to prepare hearts to receive the Living Word,"
another medley of happy praise songs.
My neighbor is a thoughtful man, a Ph.D.,

enough of a believer to value where
the worship leader's careful planning intends
to deliver the assembly. But Monday over lunch
he confided, honestly, praise songs do not
work for him. He wishes some musician
would compose a crown of lamentations
and all worship leaders would have to learn them.
Rolland is not depressed or morbid, just Welsh
and feels keenly that much is amiss

on this planet and inside his skin, so honesty
in life for him requires the same in worship.
Does he presume too much: not only
that God exists and cares about things
like our praise or lamentation, but also that I
care about anything beyond having a friend
to eat lunch with on Mondays? He could say
we are dead and living in hell, and I'd
still be there each week at our window table.

Sometimes I think he's trying to convert me.
I don't mind. I admire his believing
that all things are sustained by the ineffable
word of a resurrected, first-century rabbi, even
those things that may break God's heart.
I, too, seek a theory, a Spirit perhaps
who bears an affection for my neighbor's
five kids, the cranky super in our building,
the dreamer I have never ceased to be.

From the ends of the earth I call to you.
Psalm 61:2

THE VULTURE TREE

In Woodstock
there's a dead tree
I pass daily

that stands
in the front yard
of a white house,

entirely suburban.
Except they
roost in it—

red-beaked
turkey buzzards—
maybe twenty in all.

By 8:30 a.m.,
they're off to work.
Jesus said,

"Where vultures
gather, there
a corpse is."

Could I be
happy as
a turkey buzzard?

Would I mind
the gallows humor
and forever

being regarded
as ghastly? Consider
the bright side:

Nothing
higher on
the food chain.

Always
something dying
to be eaten.

Lowborn men are but a breath, the highborn are but a lie.
Psalm 62:9

IN IT

The news is not good. So why do I turn
to it every evening during dinner
and again at eleven before bed?
Why, when I wake up, do I want to know
what I have missed overnight?

I am a sucker for thrillers littered
with indiscreet senators, large betrayals,
honest-to-god bad guys whose bitterness
toward some neighbor has landed them
on the planet's most-wanted list.

Fiction is clever, but nobody
actually stabs or dies or gets cuckolded;
the invasion's invented, the torture
less terrible than a child de-legging an ant.
Not so the news. Even as edited,

the kidnapped are accounted for
as truly missing, our enemies train
with real ammunition, the fire that scorched
ten-thousand acres and a hillside spa—
as edited, that story, too, plays

into whatever this thing is that we
endure more or less together—*Live!*
Late-breaking!—and anything lost to the flames
is never just a symbol or narrative prop.
I turn on the news, yes, because

it is my story, the thriller I'm in—
sad and wonderful. Sad and wonderful.

I think of you through the watches of the night;
I sing in the shadow of your wings.
Psalm 63:6, 7

AGAINST NOSTALGIA

Think jazz club, 1953. Think past midnight, the casual clink of ice in glasses, between numbers the murmur of slurred conversation. And connecting each disparate dot—bartender, waitress, trumpeter, patron, bare light bulb—the slow, stratified drift of cigarette smoke. Think Birdland, Vanguard.

Or think rock ballroom, 1969, east or west, Bill Graham, the wild, feedbacking wail of distorted guitar. Think tie-dyed freaks in bellbottom blue jeans, bloodshot eyes half-closed, hallucinations of bathing naked beneath a strobing waterfall of pure sound.

No getting around whatever scene may cradle an artistic innovation, but spare us the endless revivals—Mötley Crüe at the Woodstock Fair—old fans dolled up in silly costumes, big hair. Think angel of death. Far better: the subtle tremble that signals a new music rising in the predawn dark, startling awake the singular voice.

Surely the mind and heart of man are cunning.
Psalm 64:6

OLD STORY

In my childhood place—right window,
back seat—skirting a field of waist high

yellow grass: a striped green carnival tent,
all top, no walls. I can see under, straight

through to blue sky beyond, except
where he stands, high noon light dazzling

off sweat-glazed back and shoulders, great
black arms stretched between tent poles

and resting, or perhaps—I thought at the time—
chained like Samson to the known world.

I could drive you there, a mile or two outside
the small town fifty miles outside the city

I did my best to move away from, but why
bother. The field is choked with houses.

Where morning dawns and evening fades you call forth songs of joy.
Psalm 65:8

RENTING

Forsythia. Lilac. Rhododendron.
Admirable for their tenacity
and patience between

blooms. Yet she hurries much,
does what she must:
make it to work on time,

meet all project deadlines, avoid
a boss's shit-list. Not exactly
noble, but the job

and the job's wage keep
her from indigence. Or so
the boss, a minor demiurge,

would have her believe.
What else is there?
This evening a stiff breeze

sweeps the nimble limbs
that frame the narrow half-acre
behind the white cape

she will never own. The yard.
The neighbors. Her life
among them. Those rhododendron.

He has preserved our lives.
Psalm 66:9

ANTICIPATING OUR RETIREMENT

Her plan: to visit forty-plus friends per year,
one friend a week for as many puttering years
as we may be welcomed by them. After that—
for, one by one, they will die or refuse our calls—
we will lay claim quietly to public lands:
interstate rest stops, state parks, scenic overlooks,
national seashores and wilderness areas, you name it.
This is her vision for finishing as we began,
debt-free and future-bound. No doubt you have
heard it said, "Birds have their Soho lofts;
foxes their waterfront condos." True, and true.
But we will finish up here having only the wheels
that will bear us gloriously from point A to point B.
My part: to choose the model, make, and color.

May the Gentiles be glad and sing for joy.
Psalm 67:3

FOR THE DIRECTOR OF MUSIC

In the midst of my muddle, O God,
sneak up, come alongside, break an egg
over my head. By your annoying goodness

make a royal mess of my cynicism,
provoke praise and melody and the laughter
of self-pity ribbed by grace. Bring it on,

for this would be salvation to me, tired
as I am of the cult of earnestness.
Give me the bread of gladness, and the land

will know of it, the rocks and fields will
hear it from my mouth. Though none join me,
I will not be silent. With or without

stringed instrumentation: a psalm, a song
of joy among the peoples weary of earth.

As wax melts before the flame...
Psalm 68:2

THEN

Then she knocked and without waiting entered.
      Then she tried to speak.
            Then she apologized.
Then she said
      a plane had flown into
            the World Trade Center,
a tower had fallen, and another
      plane had crashed into the Pentagon.
            Then she left the room.
Then without having to be told
      I canceled the rest of class,
            and without having to be told
we walked together to the auditorium
      where, without having to be told,
            everyone had begun to gather.
Then I saw my wife arrive
      with her class, and from across
            the auditorium I knew we were both
thinking about our son.
      Then the trustee's conference room
            became a communication center.
Then dozens of students and teachers
      donated the use of their cell phones.
            Then dozens of students and teachers
started dialing and redialing nonstop
      trying to reach family in New York City.
            Then our son,

keeping musicians hours in New York City,
        awoke. Then he dressed
                and walked up West 51st Street
to get coffee. Then crossing 8th Avenue
        he looked south
                at smoke rising over lower Manhattan.
Then my call made it through
        to our son in New York City
                as he stood without coffee
on 8th Avenue looking south.
        Then I tried to speak.
                Then I apologized.
Then I passed the cell phone to the next person.

I have come into the deep waters; the floods engulf me.
Psalm 69:1

ISOLATO

Tonight the reward for finishing a draft of his poem:
TV, some utterly brainless sitcom or anything
on a sports channel. Name it, and whatever
the show, he knows it and the advertisers
who make of it a delivery system for their message,
their juice; think seed, semen. Yes,
to watch is to get brainfucked by a team of clever
ad executives. Gang banged. This is how
he rewards himself.
               And tonight
the pennant race continues—prime-time—the series
tied at two apiece. But this is not a poem
about what he may or may not choose to watch.
This is about the work he has been given to do. *Selah.*

Hasten, O God—O Lord, do not delay.
Psalm 70:1, 5

FOR NOW

Bill can't wait
to join the angels
and Donna in paradise.

He's nearly giddy
with anticipation, all day
calling attention

to local beauty and how,
without ceasing,
it speaks of that ethereal

elsewhere, eases
the burden of exile.
With her ordeal finally

behind him, it is no longer
compelling merely
to rid the earth of fools

and idiot colleagues,
though frankly
this would still work for me.

"All good," Bill says
with a shrug and a smile.
"But what's even better? Listen.

Listen."

From the depths of the earth you will again bring me up.
Psalm 71:20

ELEGY

for Jerry Carroll

From behind a boyhood wall of rocks,
you and I lobbed pine cones at passing cars.

In cracks between other rocks, we hid the first
cigarettes we stole from our mothers' purses.

You always loved the feel of flat rocks—
stones really—in your palm, their release

and curving flight toward distant targets.
No easy, point-blank throwing for you.

In our teens at the reservoir, we jumped
from rocks—fifty feet, buck naked—

the rocks you, by then a college freshman,
tumbled from and died instantly. Last summer

in B. C., atop Blackcombe—three-hundred-
sixty degrees of treeless summits, ten

centimeters of new snow—again rocks
and the incomparable gentleness of light.

Some days I imagine it's where you've gone:
climbed to the rock center of a circle of peaks

and set your tent forever there in that gathered
community of transparency and praise.

Endow the king with your justice, O God.
Psalm 72:1

LITANY FOR AN EMPIRE

The emperor, by his own admission,
grumpy, nonanalytical,
woefully resistant
to big picture thinking
and the cries of the poor—
but, my, the castle landscaping.

Pray for the emperor.

Wouldn't be so bad
with a buffer of brilliant advisors,
but yikes! they—
a butcher, a baker,
a sleazy poll taker—see
even less of the whole than he.

Pray for the emperor's advisors.

One side of me wants the empire,
from squatters to landed lords,
to prosper, not even one
tree failing to bear fruit or stream
unwilling to cough up netfuls of fish
for the tables of the realm.

Pray for Babylon; as she prospers, we prosper.

But my notion of prosperity differs
from that of the emperor who assumes
that complaints against his nobles

mean the lazy poor must be chafing
at being made to do their work.
Please. It is not the work that chafes,

and so there is another side of me
that cannot abide his royal assemblies,
that stands with the "lazy poor"
around the perimeter of his banquet hall
and waits with those who wait
for justice to roll across the realm
like a mighty, unforgiving flood.

Yes, pray for the emperor's soul,
whose name will be forgotten
like a nondescript meal eaten in haste.
And pray for mine.

Book Three

When I tried to understand all this, it was oppressive to me.
Psalm 73:16

OFF JAKE'S PIER

Fish Point, Maine

North through the square, gull-stained arch:
lobster boats, terns, cormorants, osprey—the whole
confetti-strewn harbor—and above the far rocks
a stunning new "camp," senatorial among more
representative habitations. Been a few harsh words
among longtime locals—Jake, one of them—
resenting inelegantly how the camp's
casual grandeur alters the scale of the entire bay
and renders more and more obvious their own
homes' dull and sagging lines. Yet all this—
the point, the harbor, the new camp—inheres
from one moment to the next so perfectly
not one atom in the retina of a seal pup ever goes
suddenly missing. Why, it almost seems we are living
into a prefab universe rising immediately beneath
and around us. But more likely nothing exists
even five minutes from now, and we, along with all
things, are figures in an inscrutable *poiema*
that in each instant of becoming is not here, here,
then gone like a phrase in a jazz improvisation
sustained seamlessly over the architecture we call *time*,
and only by what we call *mind* do we grasp the immense
rhythm—and craft—of its coming in and going out.

Turn your steps toward these everlasting ruins.
Psalm 74:3

NORTH HOUSATONIC

Two decades back the state cleaned up the river.
Now, with innumerable swallows sweeping
this way and that above her light rapids,

I wade along the rocky western edge
and nod to the week's last fishermen and day-
tripping paddlers in their rented canoes.

It is good to be on holiday in Connecticut,
isn't it? And no longer at odds with how we came
by this real estate—loving our mail-order

hats, wide-brimmed and draped with fine
no-see-um netting—the late afternoon hillside
awash in the fast fade of something like alpenglow.

No one from the east or the west or from the desert can exalt a man.
Psalm 75:6

TO EXALT ONESELF (QUIETLY)

i.   Dismiss as insufficient
        the egalitarian nod of sunlight;

ii.   With one hand,
        set in motion all machinery
        as may elevate the self
        above the muddle of one's peers;

iii.   When this works, feign humility, and

iv.   With the other hand,
        engage the protocol
        for irreversible advancement
        into your pantheon of choice;

v.   When that works, retire.
        Gracefully

vi.   Disappear, averting your gaze,
        lest anyone beneath you see your eyes.

He is feared by the kings of the earth.
Psalm 76:12

ENOUGH

In a garden, one word, and a new way bursts
open in the redneck heart of a fisherman,

an old accessory of war falls, dropped
beside a severed ear, and God in the mayhem

stoops to take up again not the sword
but the ear and attend to the wounded.

Ever since God told Abraham
that He is not a deity who desires the death

of a child, the change was in the works.
And now here, in a garden,

with one word God reconstitutes
the modus operandi of his people on earth.

In an instant, blood-weariness blossoms
into rebuke—*Enough!*—and to make example

to the strong and weak, the brave and bitter
of this world, God lays down his arms.

I cried out to God for help; my soul refused to be comforted.
Psalm 77:1-2

OPENING DAY

Classes at the school where I work begin on Friday.
The newly renovated student union will teem

with teens buying books, playing air hockey, snacking
on burgers and fries from The Tuck.

A far cry from School No. 1, Beslan, North Ossetia
where last week, armed with guns, bombs,

and a short list of demands, pro-Chechen militants—
male and female Allah created them—secured

the campus—one thousand students, teachers, parents
assembled for convocation—and captured

headlines everywhere—300 dead, 700 wounded—a bold
stroke rendering frivolous the evil I plot on my bed at night.

Yet if I despair of either my fullness or their
affliction, then I succumb to what I know is a lie

but cannot name. This claims my heart: the scores
of school children fleeing through broken windows,

their captors' bullets finding them mid-flight, silencing
the light, filling up the sufferings of Christ.

I will open my mouth in parables.
Psalm 78:2

JUBILATE

Praise the parable—the story it tells—and
how it means and
what on earth it may mean and

the way we, like children, keep returning
from our well-meaning forays, ever circling back
to the broad lap of this thing or that for what may sustain us.

Praise how we keep arriving at point B
having begun typically at some point A, the wonder
of otherness being the new wine that makes our heads spin.

Beware the closed circularity of the disenchanted,
the *a priori* rule that refuses any chance
of an intersecting transcendent. Such a rule is

no rule recognizable to the story itself but
only to those whose long and short days—round and round and
round they go—will end in futility, or worse.

There is a story that is not this poem that this poem
tells nothing of, except it is a parable well worth telling and
to know it makes a difference impossible to overstate.

May the groans of the prisoners come before you.
Psalm 79:11

LESS IS MORE

Am I the only one, sick of the news
from Jerusalem, to wish the land

would vanish, all belligerents with it?
Perhaps a tear in the time-space curtain,

then—*whoosh!*—gone—West Bank, Dome
of the Rock; from the Golan Heights

to the Gaza Strip—all of it instantly
sucked off stage, removed like a wart

from a thumb, a thumb from a hand. Trust me,
I dislike collateral damage as much

as the next guy, but how long
these headlines, the inhumanity, daily

mirror of my own insufferable heart?
Here, founded on similar sand,

this house of loathing lies pitched toward
a fall that would be my future

were I to anchor myself inside its walls.
How I wish it, too, would meet with

irreversible deletion, a start to the end
of all wars against the blessedness of innocence.

Of Asaph. A psalm.
Psalm 80

E-MAILS TO ASAPH

1.

My take on what you presented in class?
Great refrain: the intimate, even fearsome

desire named by parallel verbs aching
for satisfaction—to see the face of God—

and in that moment of the poem, three times,
nothing else matters, not form or content.

2.

Sorry the class's feedback felt unfriendly,
but your peers had the good of your "psalm"

in mind, and in the end, as I said then,
the poem's final shape is wholly up to you.

3.

Yes, I reread the poem. Closely.
Another strong point,

given the supplicatory nature
of your piece: consistency of person.

Unlike many of David's psalms
that flip from first to second to third then

back to first, this one of yours
sits well, first to last,

in the second person. That said,
look again at your opening six lines

and reconsider Nicole's comment
about mixed metaphors.

4.

Fine.

If your God's good with mixed metaphors,
who am I to argue.

But for future reference:
just because you hear the poem

as a song lyric doesn't excuse you
from having to deal with issues of craft.

P.S. Drop/add ends Friday.

Begin the music, strike the tambourine.
Psalm 81:2

SING FOR JOY

Which is not as immediate as, say, supper
or as titillating as chicks or fame, but
in a sad world where, no matter how well
we eat or fuck or preen, all things tend
toward suffering and diminishment,
maybe there's nothing better to sing for
than such joy as may buoy us up,
return us to a "right mind"—

                     provided
there's something to rise or return to,
something without which we face a long
inconsequential fiction with no possible
happy ending, no hope of reinstatement
or royal lover of souls to take us back.
Broken and embittered as we are,
if we cannot sing for joy, why sing?
To show how clever we can be? How much
better than trees at making meaningless noise?

You are "gods"—you are all sons of the Most High.
Psalm 82:6

IN THE SCHOOL LIBRARY

> *A man can receive only what is given him from heaven.*
> John 3:27

After hours, he shares workspace
with a housekeeper's radio audible

throughout the building's modern,
multi-level foyer. It is tuned in

to a local station: soft rock, weather,
news, the occasional talk show.

He shares it also with a card-sized copy
of a Russian icon—the Savior's gilded

Descent into Hell—image
of the crazy hope that he keeps

on his reading chair's wide arm.
The housekeeper's name is Virginia.

His office door opens onto her domain.
Daily—he is never present for it—

she dusts, vacuums, empties
his trash and recycling, a job both

gift and embarrassment, and no matter
how variously she repositions

his papers—*every piece in its pile,
every pile in its place*—he never

feels piqued, only grateful. As when,
seeing him enter and begin the climb

to his third-floor cell, she turns down
the radio's volume. A bit, anyway.

Enough certainly for him to hear
and receive the difference.

O God, do not keep silent.
Psalm 83:1

EVEN A POSTCARD

Like, say, one of those
stupid ones with a fat couple
eating massive ice cream sundaes
on a park bench at some beach
and a rude caption like *The Bigger
the Better* on a curly blue banner
splayed across their lumpy shins,
but no, not even that. So what
was I supposed to think? You
on that Greek island all summer, I
behind the express cash register
at the same old supermarket,
and up walks your twin sister all
smiles, her cart loaded with low-carb
salt-n-vinegar soy crisps and lite
beer. So yes, her party sounded
pretty damn happening, and yes,
okay, her lips are softer than yours,
but what the hell did you expect?
That I'd get all religious about
our love, become some kind of monk
for you? Think postcard. Even one
stupid postcard.

My heart and my flesh cry out for the living God.
Psalm 84:2

BETTER FAR

I am a speck lodged in the hem of a garment,
dust in the tight weave of a fabric draped

sari-like around the divinity-beyond-imagining
whose nature limits his wardrobe to what is

of love and lovely beyond whatever we may mean
by *beautiful*. Suspended here, I am ecstatic.

Though cancer and suicide have taken friends
and former students, and ideologues everywhere

stain the air with their maniacal raving,
not a day passes without my grateful amazement

that I have not been swept from my small place
by some fastidious hand that knows a hitch-

hiking piece of lint from an integral thread.
Better far this hour than never to have been.

Faithfulness springs forth from the earth.
Psalm 85:11

GLORY

Seems the ground knows when to begin—
October, October—pulling on the dark

dugs of this good forest, and year to year
you and I, bundled against the chilling air,

draw close to hear the suckling and smell
the sweet milk of wet, fallen leaves.

Consider the earth, and think faithfulness—
a tilted planet rounding its solar course.

This year our steps are slower, our hearts
distracted by a flooded basement apartment,

a goddaughter's recovery from a coma.
So we promise ourselves: next October

we will get outside more, attend more fully
to the woodland's face flush with self-offering.

HERE, NOW

I wish
the indistinct voices

across this lobby
were charged with amazement

at the miracle of being.
What harm would it do?

And that,
listening, they heard this rain's infinite

polyrhythms as metaphor
of an infinite delight

in a universe of infinite particulars.
What possible harm?

The Lord will write in the register, "This one was born in Zion."
Psalm 87:6

HUNGER

They laughed—
packed in a lockered hallway,
fisted first snow flying like blown
kisses—and looked at each other as if
nothing in the world
could possibly separate them: the first
circle I ever wanted into.

Then there was that soccer team.
Then those quiet painters in art class
whose work shook my bones loose. Then
the shaggy six in long wool coats who smoked
hashish, wrote poems, and made by hand
their underground magazine;
like a stray pup desperate for a pack,
I would make their seventh.

Which is simply to want a place, a chair
in the circle and not be a fraud.
This would be hell:
to want and want, like an unignited wick,
and die wanting, an old dog at the door
and no one home, the house
abandoned.

I am set apart with the dead.
Psalm 88:5

MY SPIRITUAL PRACTICE

When I sit still in my office for ten minutes,
the lights turn themselves off. I love being

overlooked first by the lights' motion sensors,
then by those who assume I would not choose

to sit alone in a darkened room. They pass by
looking for me elsewhere. I do not care

to be seen by anyone. I am never tempted to wave
an arm and trip the affirmational switch.

Invisibility suits me. I enjoy imagining others
deciding I must be out sick or on an errand

or that finally I've delivered on my threat: to buy
a one-way bus ticket anywhere south and west

of this office in this suburban private school
where, several times a day, I make the lights go out.

Who in the skies above can compare with the Lord?
Psalm 89:6

LAST SUNDAY IN PENTECOST

A broad shadow angles
    across the back field—
        proprietary buzzard
            sweeping bare treetops.

I thrive in late November.
    Though wars and rumors
        of wars and all things turn
            from bad to worse—this:

a warm, clear morning,
    the breeze and sunlight
        practically Caribbean,
            the bird shadow, pelican.

Book Four

All our days pass away under your wrath.
Psalm 90:9

THE GOOD LIFE

according to ARCHITECTURAL DIGEST

In a tall, open-walled poolside pagoda,
      suspended from teak rafters smooth as marble,
          saffron curtains like festal banners descend

in waves from a sweeping, hand-carved canopy
      that once topped a Buddhist temple in Thailand.
          So much for reverence in south Florida.

Some days I want out of this modern mishmash,
      this hang-loose apotheosis of the *au curant*.
          But where to go? The same

irreverence travels with me, clings to my every
      move like Spanish moss in the live oaks surrounding
          the redeployed pagoda, and I want

that pool house, pool, those lawns and live oaks,
      the uniformed staff of twenty-five smiling Cubans
          who minister like spirits to the elect of God.

You will tread upon the lion ad the cobra.
Psalm 91:13

ALISON

Their daughter, twenty-three—a depth charge—
does not like to be "fucked with" by insurance agents,

the media, presidents in pinstripes who, like sub-
marines running deep, assume they are safe

from the shallow grievances of ordinary citizens.
But she is not afraid of dying well, of descending

through the half-light with her weighted payload.
A lover of poetry and the lyrics of Radiohead,

none of her favorite verses make any sense,
though she can recite them from memory

as if they were nursery rhymes or quotations
from Chairman Mao. On the morning she explodes—

this is not a question of if but when—

their nonsense will be on her lips the way prayer
will be on mine. The difference between us:

she longs to behold the suffering of the wicked.
More and more, I have no desire that any should perish.

My horn shalt thou exalt like the horn of an unicorn.
Psalm 92:10

VISITING BROOKLYN

I dreamt of flying low above a herd
of unicorns moving rapidly through a tight,
deciduous forest. That morning when I shared
the dream with my son, he asked—ever
the audiophile—"Did their hooves thunder?"
All I remember: not one animal was white
and horse-like, but closer to the ground,
razorback, with broad hips and shoulders;
their fabled horns were not the slender lances
of medieval tapestry, but rounded protuberances
of yellow bone; and somehow I understood
my welfare rested on staying with the quick-
turning herd, hardly knowing what this means:
Lord, exalt his horn like that of a unicorn.

The world is firmly established; it cannot be moved.
Psalm 93:1

A CHRISTMAS POEM

for Roy

The surgeon did not plan on nicking
your carotid artery or spending
the holiday contemplating suicide.
The last report I received from Judy,
wife of your cousin Paul: the next
seventy-two hours are critical.
Will you wake from your coma alert
or something less than yourself?
You have two daughters—will they
grow up not knowing you? Judy said
that your family is big into God
and you are an elder in the church.
Then you understand, no doubt, how
your sudden condition, the simple
effect of accident, has an incisive way
of disturbing the theological peace
of those who are comfortable in Zion.
The Lord reigns. Yes. True. But
this happens, and now you lie there,
as lively as a lawn in December.
Me, I'm itching for a few easy answers.
Like "God is love." Or "This, too,
is your path." Or "The Lord giveth,
the Lord taketh away; blessed be. . . ."
Galled and itching to lay waste all such
comfort as may be neatly swaddled

in the hasty brocade of piety. Sadness
is the province we inhabit: tundra,
endless cloud cover, precious little light.

"My foot is slipping."
Psalm 94:18

GENUINE REPLICATIONS

The pitch in the subject line being for neither
pharmaceuticals nor porn but watches,
this morning I decided to open the SPAM.
Good news: the watches are not those fake
knock-offs any tourist can pick up cheap
on a big-city sidewalk, but honest-to-goodness
replicas, authentic pieces of jewelry that cost
a tad more, but you know what you're paying for:
peace of mind, that feeling you know and trust.
Language is not the enemy here any more
than industry is the enemy or government.
When I consider the immense and terrible
perfection of a class-five hurricane, the purity
of a tsunami, or a quark's thrilling song and dance,
I do not comprehend how anything perverse
ever could have evolved anywhere in the universe.
That you and I exist at all makes no sense:
from primal forces dumb as the chair I sit on
rises sentient personality? Not likely.
And not just sentient but sniveling and self-
absorbed, arrogant and pathologically cruel.
Explain this: I feel ashamed of my own kind.
Some humans are even bored, determined,
it would seem, to prove that they are also stupid.
On some mornings it is easier to believe
nonsense will resolve into meaning and God
will pay back the wicked what they deserve.
But this is not one of those mornings.

In his hand are all the corners of the earth.
Psalm 95:4

A WINTER SEA

Bill's camera rests in my lap.
He is walking alone up the beach he and Donna

would visit each New Years Day.
The wind is cold. There is no snow. No surf.

This is the first anniversary of her death.
He has asked me not to take a picture of him among

the dozen or so couples out for a stroll.
I snap a few shots of a white horse and rider stopped

before a shoeless girl on tiptoe, nose to nose
with the steaming mare. The little girl must be freezing.

When the day's prints return from the lab,
I hope he will forgive me.

Worship the Lord in the beauty of holiness.
Psalm 96:12

WHAT HOLDS US BACK

The Lord reigns,
    let the earth be glad—
        and Sunday to Sunday says

it's about a body: mind-
    house, love-pump, engine
        of desire. Was he or was he not

human? Did he or did he not
    rise from death? Sunday
        to Sunday, if about nothing

else, then: a body's flesh,
    blood, bones, veins, teeth,
        the whole vast prairie of nerves,

topography of parts, seemly
    and unseemly. Was he
        or was he not all that we are

and more? Beyond merely
    good, his earth-gift, being
        for the body—yours, mine—

declares our bodies good
    beyond imagining, and how
        we receive it says whether

a body, having died
      and changed to be like
           his body, passes on from this

thinning coil to that thief-
      thick Paradise where he
           has gone before and now is.

*

What holds us back:
      the foolish things we do
           in the body, always in the body

yielding to lust or anger,
      the gravities of unbelief.
           Even the least foolish thing.

The mountains melt like wax before the Lord of all the earth.
Psalm 97:5

YOU ARE GOLIATH

The stone is flying at your head,
and if you cannot dodge quickly enough
or deflect it with a brain pulse,
what's the harm in yelling, *Become bread*?
This may make no difference
to the stone, but what if—and flash,
it's a tiny loaf that hits you like an edible
doll pillow, and the doughy thump
to your noggin makes you blink,
but there's no pain, no blood,
and recovering instantly, you notice
across the way the kid's jaw drop—his aim
had been perfect—slack as the sling
in his hand, and you realize that stories
can have unexpected endings.
Whole histories can turn on a word.
And you smile wryly the moment before—
did you doubt that a low-tech enemy
could prevail against you?—
a smooth, well-aimed stone crashes
against the high tower of your forehead.

He has done marvelous things.
Psalm 98:1

AFTER A SNOWFALL

Above a shapeless field, the fine, up-swept tip of a redtail's wing.
On an unplowed road, euphoria at spotting it suddenly.
Then later over tea, delight in recalling the moment's perfection.
And now this.
            If all were mere necessity, then why such beauty?
We are perhaps the only witness to what we think we see
and long to enter—a sacred grove, a new earth, a father's well-
prepared welcome home—and so leave behind all want, all sorrow
for what never fails to spoil our truest effort.
            My wish:
to hold close the wide, miraculous world I lumber through
shouting, *There!* and *Over here!* or waving subtly whenever
words or sudden motion might send it fleeing—everywhere rejoicing.

Worship at his holy mountain.
Psalm 99:9

THE OBLATION

Blackcombe, British Columbia

Delivered by chairlift, surrounded
by sundeck and sitting at a walnut-
stained picnic table, I had come
for the rugged, rock-peaked horizon
of the Coastal Range—and now these
ten centimeters of overnight snow.
Did I say it was July? And yet
what snuck up and claimed my attention?
A black she-bear who lumbered
into the clearing just below the summit café,
her snout probing the slope's rough-cut
grasses and low shrubs for anything edible.
It is one thing to approach large nature
telescopically, quite another
to have large nature take an interest
in your cheeze nachos. I had read
and re-read the tourist's wildlife guide
and listened closely to the day-hike staffer
review the likelihood of encounter:
what to do if. . . , when. . . . Hey, I'm good
with possibilities that lack a pulse
or body temperature, the hypothetical carnivore
that hasn't dirty claws or yellow teeth;
when you consider her
there's nothing categorical in her eyes.

But what looked up at my nachos, at me, then
back at my nachos was neither hypothetical
nor some toothless stunt bear in a carnival sideshow.
And as she rose on her hind quarters
for a better look at my six dollar snack,
I felt the universe, in a calm, subsonic whisper,
invite my participation in the practice
of nonattachment. Never
more motivated to be spiritual,
I lifted slowly the flimsy white paper bowl out
over the edge of the sundeck—a deal
is a deal—and tipped it, releasing a clumped
wad of corn chips into thin, mountaintop air.

We are the sheep of his pasture.
Psalm 100:3

IN THE RIGHT DIRECTION

There is shouting, and then there's shouting
for joy. I don't believe, having grown up

a card-carrying member of the library caste—
"quiet society"—that I have ever done either, though

the day that editor said yes to my Thanksgiving rewrite,
I yelped and sank my teeth ram-like into my wife's derriere.

I will have nothing to do with evil.
Psalm 101:4

NO VILE THING

At a sister boarding school, lice: body, head,
and pubis. One rich girl's dreads infested,

they estimated, with maybe two-thousand
resilient nits per natty lock. Her daddy had her

driven to a clinic where, once shorn and shaved,
they dipped her, so I heard, in malathion.

Though inconvenient and socially embarrassing,
it is not difficult to delouse a human body.

Foul surfaces, too, can be scraped, scoured, white-
washed, stripped, bleached, repainted. There's hope

for soulless things, nothing a little money
and cleverness can't cook up to restore a right

appearance for whatever has lost its sheen.
But what hope for those who long for more

than a reclamation of unseemly exteriors?
For, say, the ripping of envy from an old heart

or for such love as is quick to take measures
sufficient to cure a soul? The girl's body

will return to a dorm room made new, the clean
form return to function. And what then? What bath

to restore the good dream, such high regard
for all things, all people, that we may see God?

INSOMNIAC'S COMMISSION

One desert owl among ruins, alone
on a housetop—it is my job

to take this census of what remains
since the bombing stopped.

If I had been able to sleep,
if I had not taken a walk through town,

I never would have known
she was here, her cries, her dark

profile beautiful above
the silence of this god-awful place of dust

and wind-scattered ashes.
In the morning, I will fold up camp,

file my ridiculous report,
move on to the next empty village.

All my inmost being, praise his holy name.
Psalm 103:1

DIRECT ADDRESS

Odd the way King David spoke to himself—
Praise the Lord, O my soul—in the imperative,

the way he spoke to angels and the works
of God's hands—*Praise the Lord, you his angels*

and all his works everywhere—as if, without
his speaking it, they would not join the chorus.

Ah, conviction! Yet address one's self, one's soul?
In the popular sense of the word, wholly

schizo: David speaking, so it seems, across
some deep, internal divide or through, say,

a locked door, and I'm not sure who's inside—
the soul or the speaker—and who is out,

or whether David's soul ever spoke back,
told him, in the imperative, to *shut up* or *bug off.*

The birds of the air nest by the waters.
Psalm 104:12

MORNING

Clothed in light, stripped
to creative will and wisdom's

unerring eye for detail, he looks
over the earth—wind and aspen,

eagle and prairie, river
and wild horse—and, bride-like,

she trembles under his gaze.
In the early chapters, you and I

are henna on her slender neck
and ankles, a string of pearls

between her breasts, a gold
thread slung low across her wide

hips and belly. No reason yet
to wonder at our being here.

To you I will give the land.
Psalm 105:11

SHORT LIST OF WONDERS, BESIDES THAT SUMMER SUNRISE FROM THE TRAIN IN NORTH DAKOTA: SKY, HORIZON, PRAIRIE

In a winter-flattened wheat field, the hundred or so
wild turkeys I mistook, at first glance, for geese.

Facing east, the sky in Connecticut a half-hour past
sunset—infinite cobalt glaze, pearl-gray moon.

This desire: for grace upon ridiculous grace to lighten
the solitary heart of my one child now grown up.

And this, too: the inscrutable furnace that warms
my rooms, her iron pipes fussing endlessly over nothing.

They exchanged their Glory for an image of a bull.
Psalm 106:20

PORNEA

What can you do? Maybe distract
the skinny boyfriend who keeps her
plied with heroin? Maybe wrap
her nodding body in your overcoat
and hide her in the back seat
of your car out behind the café?
And why not save him, too? Restore
thirty pounds, wash off the makeup.
Everything's a mess and you're
tired of tawdry—so many captives
of the lie, the needle—and you want
a good future for the sad addict
that her idiot boyfriend can't begin
to comprehend. But she wants
him, another fix, and couldn't
care less about the award-winning
film you want them both to see.

Book Five

Some wandered in desert wastelands.
Psalm 107:4

GOOD THINGS

At the Met, hundreds of instruments locked
behind bulletproof glass—Segovia's

among them—cold as a photograph.
When I get home, Bill will be dropping by

whose life, one year beyond Donna's slow
dying, has begun to open into what is,

for him, a familiar direction. For years
the road was his destination of choice:

bars, honky-tonks, county fairs; *anywhere,
any time, any amount*; every now

and then a real music hall, a listening
crowd with sober ears who cared how he voiced

the light, bending twang of his pedal steel.
Just back from the first tour in a decade—

eight shows in eight nights, from Cincinnati
to Atlanta—Bill says he has stories.

So I'm guessing, over coffee we'll do
a fair bit of laughing, settle into

that crazy sense of knowing why we're here,
then maybe say a prayer or two before

he returns to an empty apartment
and I flick the toggle on my Blues Junior,

wait for the tubes to begin to glow, and send
the first notes of a new song spinning.

I will measure off the Valley of Succoth.
Psalm 108:7

LINING THE FIELD

To contain the action, delineate
in and out of bounds, the hourly crew

paints with a water-based white paint the well-
plotted, regulation perimeter

of the boys lacrosse field. I watch from this
third floor classroom and think of my mother,

a school girl in British Columbia,
learning the game from an Okanogan

whose ancestors received it as a gift
with one rule of play: play to win

with such vigor as befits
gratitude to the One who is

giver, spectator, and referee—
and he may restore gladness, heal the sick.

From this room, my skybox I call it, I
cannot tell whose cold fingers tie and untie

the string stretched between stakes hammer-driven
in the still frozen corners of the field,

or whose gloves grip the cumbersome machine
that sprays on the paint; they will receive

their reward. And rain or shine, teams
will compete unaware of who watches them.

Let them know that it is your hand.
Psalm 109:27

AGAINST COMPLAINING

This blind is for birders, the land a trust,
the pair of Hooded Mergansers a sight

for eyes sore from clearing e-mails, feigning
interest in one-sided conversations.

Though glad for the company, solitude
like grief encloses him. Whether in this

hut or at a lunch table with colleagues,
Bill sits *shiv'ah* for all who, in the end,

will have refused the grace of morning light
on reeds, the warm scent of loam at midday,

the peepers' evensong. Poor and needy
is not how he describes himself, but rich

beyond imagining. I sit with him
and, back and forth, share the binoculars.

You will receive the dew of your youth.
Psalm 110:3

PENTECOST

for DLD

She and I await the Ruby-throateds' return,
and as we watch, paper wasps
have begun to strip our cedar porch rails;
chimney swifts, back already
from the headwaters of the Amazon,
swim laps in the silvering, late-afternoon air.
Nothing new here, not the wait nor
the want to make new whatever may
make burdensome—or grievous—
this ecstatic season. Not even this
old art. But more than tongues
or hummingbirds or art, we await,
beyond wasp and swift or even want,
a word to set ablaze the air, ignite our hearts.

Great are the works of the Lord.
Psalm 111:2

BETWEEN

An astrophysicist studies effects
the psalmist declares are works of a king.

The bee sunning beside me on the bench
is no fool and serves without resistance.

Good will come to him who is generous.
Psalm 112:5

IN COOPERSTOWN

for Drum Hadley

He wants to show me,
before nightfall, something
to take with me into sleep,
so we walk upstream,
up the laddered notch behind
a high-minded bird dog
released from a firm heel.

Here, at his family's old
summer place, the names
of things have become for him
harder to recall—neckerchief,
cellar stairs, corkscrew—
the most simple chores
more difficult to perform.

Later, by the fire, he will say
he'd also love to show me
the canyons of the borderlands,
where Spanish Dagger
blooms on the ridgelines
and he trusts his cutting horse
to remember what he cannot.

But here, along this narrow creek,
that conversation waits
until he has sent me ahead

to crest the next steep rise,
wade a shallow bend
in the stream and step into
Cooper's Gorge alone—there,

beyond his call or whistle,
mist blackens the south
wall's rock face, and yellow
leaves collect the day's last
light, hold on through dusk,
a thousand thin lanterns
suspending around my head.

The Lord stoops down to look on the heavens and the earth.
Psalm 113:6

INTERCESSION

On the river, Emily, a senior
dropped to third boat without the courtesy

of a reason, recovers silently
in her new seat, grateful for the rain.

Outside this poem, over the nations, far
above the heavens and the earth, what?

It happens: even at a private school
on the water in a crew shell, the child's

heart, panning for a golden word,
sifts the day's runoff and returns empty.

She will be seated with princes, by God.
Am I praying this or demanding it?

Wherever You are, assuming You are,
do better than stoop to look. Raise her up.

Tremble, O earth, at the presence of the Lord.
Psalm 114:7

ENTER GOD

Ah, those glassy nights I start to feel
with Stevie Ray those blues I've no right

to feel, but out they flow like someone's blood,
not mine, not mine. Like someone's blood, not mine.

And that's about how long the feeling lasts.
Rain tonight. A light, roof-top percussion.

What if, like that Stevie Ray feeling, God
were to pay us a visit one evening,

come to our campus unannounced, and take up
residence on the quad behind the dorms?

Would the valley below the tennis courts
be exalted, the hills beyond the rink

brought low? Children of the Upper East Side—
would they skip like lambs, dance like King David

before the ark of the Lord? Bring it on.
Roll in, sweet chariot. Swing down and rock us

deep with some dark shuffle of transcendence.
In the meantime, I'll take my SRV cranked.

It is not the dead who praise the Lord.
Psalm 115:17

FROM THE GREEN ROOM

They all want to be entertained, fooled
into feeling pretty-much fine about

the price of admission. The only art
that matters: delivering better than

they expect of just what they're looking for.
Infundibular leaps to mind, the round

and round of fecally-enriched toilet
water en route to a sunless sea.

Tonight the venue bears a resemblance
to Sheol, the miles behind me

a precipitous, roots country descent.
If this were Oz, I'd click my ruby heels

and bless God for Kansas. As it is,
I will play the gig, collect half the door,

crash in my Chevy's back seat, and maybe
tomorrow, if I'm still alive, call it quits.

The cords of death entangled me.
Psalm 116:3

THE CENTERFIELDER

Despite a mitt the width of his torso,
the ball skipped by him into left center.

Just a little pre-game fielding practice,
yet parents have eyes—and the other team.

I saw him pivot, the curved bill of his blue
cap shielding his face, to give it chase.

But that's all I saw. I was driving, and
the road owned my worship. Okay, maybe

the quality of his pain fails to rise
above the level of little league shame.

Maybe I should not have dragged him into
this middle-brow sonnet. Can I help it

that I played his position? What is death
if not the knowledge of having fucked up?

GAMBOL

If, as the smarty-pants declare, there is
no One to whom the word *God* refers,

nor therefore a Christ who is *Light of Light,*
very God of very God, then I am

a big dummy to believe that God is
and that he rewards those who seek him.

What I want to know is how the party
of smarty-pants can be so sure they know

what they say they know they know. Believe me,
I crave their confidence, or should I say

omniscience, for only the god-like
can be so sure that such a thing as God

does not exist. On the off chance, however,
that their science is insufficiently

omni to justify the grand assumption,
I will continue to believe in God,

that is, in the likelihood God exists
and that this child-like hope is a cool thing,

where *cool* means perfect, ineffable,
and *thing* means gift, like a birthday present.

He has made his light shine upon us.
Psalm 118:27

SPRING COLORS

Her name is Lisa. Only fourteen months
since Donna died. Is Bill at it again

already? Who am I to judge the man?
He has a new heart. It is the first time

in his life he can remember waking
with enthusiasm for being here.

When school's done in June, his contract expires.
We've already signed and delivered ours.

Good news: though he'll be on tour all summer,
Bill's not leaving the area just yet.

He wants to bring Lisa along Thursday
when the prayer group meets in our living room.

Why do I jump so quickly to conclusions?
Spring has never been so long this subtle.

WORDS THAT MATTER

What we do: say goodbye to things
and our words for things—the sharp chatter

of a sparrow thrilling in the lilac,
a lawn mower's gruff, mechanical drone—

things and words which when forgotten
entire worlds disappear.

But this is not a song to some long-gone
gadget, say, the dial telephone. Words

that matter honor things that endure
in spite of the obsolescence of all

other things. Therefore, I sing your soul
and mine that are entirely unlike

penny candies or Studebakers.
I sing an infinite Word who calls forth

in our souls an infinite longing.
Though death may require a dislocation

of the self from all that is not the self,
this is the Word that will return us to

our right minds, a right regard for all things.
This is the Word that will wake us from death.

Save me, O Lord, from deceitful tongues.
Psalm 120:2

SONG OF ASCENTS

I love the climb, working against
gravity, selecting my line, choosing

each new pitch with attention to my knees,
happy to exult in the subtle

joys of will and pace. Not so the return.
Once I ran down mountains, leaping

scree fields, gravity the exhilarant
I would release into. But now, injuries

having exacted their gradual toll,
I prefer a chair lift. Better yet, leave

me on the peak, for worse than descending
is the Valley of the Lie where I live,

where, to prepare for a presidential
visit to Tbilisi, U.S. taxpayers

shelled out millions to have the boulevard,
from airstrip to five-star hotel, paved

and every last home and business
along Motorcade Way painted like new.

Why? Because Georgia is a model of reform,
and the world is watching on CNN,

and truth is a game played with slogans:
toilet bowl scrub brought to you by Nietzsche,

Foucault, Derrida in business suits.
Call me a fool or whatever you want,

I am ready for my final ascent,
a slow, patient extraction of the self

from the deceitful tents of Kedar,
and any approach will do.

The Lord will watch over your life.
Psalm 121:7

AT A BOARDING SCHOOL REUNION

Around the perimeter of the old chapel's interior—
I will lift up mine eyes to the hills—carved
in oak, the full text of Psalm One-Hundred Twenty-One.

What did I know, growing up in large-lawned Connecticut,
of Middle Eastern wilderness or the dangerous lines
of ascent for pilgrims going up to Jerusalem?

"Lions and tigers and bears, O my!" Yes, and bandits
and dehydration and the murderous
betrayals of weather. How could I have known

at the club, on the ball field, in the family pew—*from whence
cometh my help?*—Israel's fear of falling short of the courts of praise,
the need of grace for any success at all.

But I knew the wizard's right hand holy man
who dodged the questions we confirmands fired at him.
Why, I even served at his high altar. Nothing to it.

Now, back in this faux-Norman chapel—talk about large lawns
and *going out and coming in*—I am decades disconnected
from the sweet, sad religion of my boyhood

and slowly making peace with the difficult distance
between me and the God Nietzsche nixed,
the One we never seriously imagined was there—and worthy.

Our feet are standing in your gates, O Jerusalem.
Psalm 122:2

WILD BLUE

Though I prefer the g-force of takeoff
        to, on landing, the brakes' forward shove,
                it is more blessed to arrive than depart.

Which is not to belittle departures
        or, for the flight's duration, the Zen
                of being the airborne bird. I love a good

journey as much as the next guy. But why
        travel if not to arrive somewhere? Why
                even get out of bed in the morning?

One philosopher calls our being here
        a spasm between two oblivions,
                from lift off to touch down, all meaningless.

Nuts to that! I'll take the crazy hope
        of landing in a better country—the better
                dream—over terminal moping any day.

Have mercy, O Lord, have mercy.
Psalm 123:3

HISTORY

I didn't think to clear it—no
reason to cover my tracks—
so you found the link, *How to
Unsnap a Bra*, standing out
on yesterday's browsing history
like a new student in the front row.
The two-minute video was not
on my to-do list; the original
e-mail promised a laugh
and the link delivered me
to a menu with a wild range
of options. The category: "Self-
help." The tone: humorous. But like
so much that's never equal
to its billing—a mailbox filled
with new messages—the footage
was neither funny nor (and here
I'm twelve again, the riddle
of that clasp yet unsolved) the least
bit helpful. So damn easy
to waste time! And had we
a history button on our foreheads
that, when touched or kissed
or punched, sent a scrollable
menu across our cheeks—
obsessions on display—we'd

never again show our mugs in public.
Yes, I am guilty. I watched
the video. At least, most of it.
And yes, I could have been
outside or folding the laundry
or doing just about anything else
and I'd have been far better
occupied. But no excuses. Not one.

We have escaped like a bird out of the fowler's snare.
Psalm 124:7

1963

Each November, for as long as I lived
in our town, Stanley Flink called to collect
the shirt sizes of his best friends' growing boys
and, come Christmas Day, hand-deliver
from Brooks Brothers' mid-town branch as many
pink, button-down Oxford shirts. I remember
him—thin, dark-haired, intense—always
a sweater draped over his shoulders, the arms
tied loosely across an all-cotton chest.
Never rude to his face, we boys pegged him
for a dandy, though that's not the word we used.
Patchwork madras shorts, seersucker suits,
pastel Lily jeans, the man was a poster child
on a mission, and we were his mission field.

    Truth be told, it had been years
since I'd thought of him, but for my fiftieth,
my mother, selecting one gift per decade,
thought a pink, button-down shirt from Brooks
would be just the thing to say *The Sixties*,
as if the serial horror of the Bay of Pigs,
Bull Connor, Viet Nam never made landfall
in our suburb—*Next Station to Heaven*—where
Stanley lived and moved and knew my shirt size.
I still cannot figure out what his deal was,
whether terminally weird "that way" or just
completely out of it. Did he even notice
the ruin of our lives? Without fail—think JFK's
head exploding—Flink dressed us in pink.

The Lord surrounds his people.
Psalm 125:2

TRUE

This is bullshit:
Those who trust in Him

cannot be shaken.
Set confidence here,

and when the bough
breaks, cradle

crashes, whiplash
will not begin

to describe the anguish
of the faithful.

"Do not think disaster
cannot touch you"—

what I say to myself
on the good days.

We were like those who dreamed.
Psalm 126:1

GOOGLE *ROBIN NEEDHAM*

for Lucy et al.

Your e-mail's subject line read *Clearing*.
(How soon will this language be obsolete?)

I pictured the six of you arm-in-arm
outside your home in Katmandu, mountains

over your shoulders, the latest monsoon
making a welcome but fitful exit.

Here, a half-dozen chimney swifts cavort
above my neighbors' roof, oblivious

to the suffering you have called home
for three decades, your tent pitched among

refugees—Kampuchea, Bangladesh,
Kenya—your witness, even through the years

we lost touch, an icon of the good dream.
You are moving again, and while clearing

out boxes from closets, you found my letter,
dated, and new e-mail address and so

thought to bring me up to speed. Has it been
a year since I wrote to you? But then

your second paragraph. I had to read it
three times before I could receive its news:

the six of you on holiday in Thailand,
the twins and boys trading laugh-out-loud tales

of college life and school in Chiang Mai, all
settled in at Golden Buddha Beach.

Which is when, like Herod's goons in Bedlam,
the Christmas tsunami tore into you.

"Life is strange," you wrote. "The children ran
for their lives. I survived. And Robin, well,

google *Robin Needham*." So I did.
Now, in these ridiculous lines—his body

found after five days by Nat, your oldest,
a full kilometer into the jungle—I

cut a path through the dense tangle of crap
in my psyche to the wide open place

where all our long silences—wanted
and unwanted—converge and embrace.

In vain you rise early and stay up late.
Psalm 127:2

A WATCHMAN'S SONG

1.

How many sons to build a city—
neighborhoods, markets and parks, a palace?

And how many generations
to defend it? My hand on this hilt.

2.

Necessity peels from cedar porch rails
to frame chambered, gray paper birthing bays.

Necessity winds those same rails, erupts
into red clusters and honey-sweet air.

In a hillside grove, necessity stands
on hind legs sampling soft, young leaves.

3.

Was it necessity in the beginning
God created? And now necessity

my place on this high wall? I've had enough.
A palace, a city dump: no difference.

Your sons will be like olive shoots around your table.
Psalm 128:3

PHILIA

What the planet does: make noise—burp
of geothermal mud holes, sneeze of surf,

long, low tectonic groan of shifting plates.
And not only noise, but odors.

A boyhood favorite: hydrogen sulfide,
the gas of slick tidal pluff from the broad

marshes of the Ashley below Charleston.
Unfit for perfumery, the scent,

dark and rank, just the primal stuff
over which a pirate pair of slingshot boys—

Jack and I—might improvise a friendship,
the whole known world taking shape around them.

This, too, is what the planet does, over
and over: prove itself love's best ally.

Like grass. . . , which withers before it can grow.
Psalm 129:6

AT ELY

In a thin shadow between buttresses,
chavs pass a cigarette among themselves.

We are just off the busses, three hundred
of us crossing the lawn for Evensong.

I know to call them chavs because Allyn,
an Oxford undergraduate, taught us

the latest pejorative for low class
English white kids with nothing to live for

but trouble's wild rush of adrenaline.
In less than an hour, during the choir's over-long

antiphonal anthem and just before
the Lord Bishop stands to speak, I will nod off—

and the chavs will follow hunger into town,
every angel and archangel with them.

My soul waits for the Lord.
Psalm 130:6

COFFEE WITH VISHNU

She didn't object. His t-shirt
read *Vishnu* above the number
twenty-three, white letters
on a tangerine field, softball
no doubt. Christ, a god
at the Greenpoint Coffee House!
Took a seat at her sidewalk table
as if he knew her, though
the twitch in her smile
said not to her knowledge.
But who can refuse a Hindu deity—
hair like a waterfall at midnight,
eyes bright as deep space, a voice
to give life to the dead?
In no time: laughter and her Pit
Bull's head in his lap and his
hands kneading that muscular neck.
When my brunch arrived
with its bowl of stir fried bacon,
I must have drifted off, never
saw them leave together. Left me,
all of a sudden, feeling, *Why not me?*

My eyes are not haughty.
Psalm 131:1

WHAT I SAW

along the Methow River

1.

Late night in Winthrop, a shirtless nephew
swaggers through cameras, vintage Chevys—

it is good, by god, to be a sophomore—
glacier-styled sunglasses doing their job.

2.

This morning at their stream-side hacienda,
ridge ablaze, the same nephew, still shirtless,

watches from the porch swing: his father—
knee-deep, same glasses—casting for steelies.

3.

Morning and evening, a Bald Eagle slips by
this bend in the river, white head keen

on clear water—still pools, subtle riffles—
wholly unmindful of its brilliant tail feathers.

QUIET WORDS

Tomorrow we die. Nothing better: this
easy morning above Puget Sound, mist

obscuring Olympia. It is always
tomorrow when we die, as tomorrow

we get rich, own property, or pull up
stakes and move somewhere like this: near

water, the mountains, a university.
Tomorrow death, and there will be—*poof*—

no more weddings, diets, religious wars.
Will I be happy then? Yes, so happy,

and the garden in which I am dying
tomorrow will win garden club awards.

Nothing better: this view from a lawn chair,
ferries coming and going on the Sound.

NOTE TO BOOKSTORE OWNERS

In theory, and at its best, poetry
exalts the wide mother tongue the way

a tidal pool exalts the wide ocean
beyond. And this is not just about sales

or sour grapes or shelf-envy; cookbooks
and blockbuster beach novels will always

move more units, top the bestseller lists.
Who has ever heard of a bidding war

over movie rights to a book of poems?
But is there higher praise than *poetic?*

So why not, near the front door, a poetry
table with rotating titles, a wild mix

of styles. Think tidal pool: minnows, star-
fish, anemones, barnacles, blue crabs.

May the Maker of heaven and earth bless you.
Psalm 134:3

COMMON AS AIR

When Mrs. Weiss told us in earth science,
a light, limb-filtered breeze blessing us
through the room's west wall windows,
that somewhere camouflaged within
our every lung-full of air marches air

Hitler breathed and Khrushchev and
Richard Speck, I began breathing less—
shorter intakes, pauses after each exhale—
willing to endure panicky bursts of craving
in exchange for reducing the likelihood

of those radioactive atoms passing
from lung to blood to brain. If she included
mention of the Buddha or Madame Curie,
I do not remember it. Terror is air-borne.
And though I have been slow to believe,

so are wisdom and beauty, the breath
of canticle and rain forest, and in such
measure as dwarfs the one or two
dark, burrowing parts per million of all
that is our phenomenal inheritance. How

I wish now a teacher had told us that this
is the reason, when we hyperventilate,
we get so dizzy—so much goodness
flooding our little brains it very nearly
bowls us over, tips us toward our knees.

Those who make idols will be like them.
Psalm 135:18

PRAISE HIM

As for idols, they are impotent. Not
one can see or speak or feel

a neighbor's ache—her dog dead
and child missing below the levee. I read

the headlines and feel more
than all the idols that ever were.

Even the idol that is our idea
of God is impotent—B is not A—

yet God does what he pleases,
the earth what is true to its nature.

We build cities and pay scant attention
to either, then cry foul when the dam breaks.

Idols cannot save, nor theologies.
Only God, and that is no great comfort.

HOLY, HOLY

Before old growth: original growth.
Wonder upon wonder, and all a gift—

the wild and welcoming contours of earth,
the greater and lesser lights suspending.

The more I eat of this body, the more
unfit I am for mean allegiances;

the more I drink from this cup, the less
I desire the fellowship of lawyers.

Yet despite good growth, familiar loathing
escalates against a wicked man whose

bum leg I'd be glad to remove for him.
So it appears I must go deeper—drop

anchor-like through the old, dark phosphors
of indignance—to original light.

Blessed is he who seizes your infants and dashes them against the rocks.
Psalm 137:1

SMOKE

I have heard it said aloud—*how I wish
she would die*—though never yet to her face.

And death would be a mercy, as those she
has made to suffer most would have her live long,

suffer much. *May the thin-lipped bitch
see her towheaded darlings disemboweled*

and fed to crows. Daily, I am amazed
one woman inspires such antipathy.

Worse, Nebuchadnezzar knows her heavy hand
and praises her. So now, who deserves

death more? She who sets the fires, they who've been
burned and burn with hate, or the one who—

between the Tigris and Euphrates—
pays the arsonist her wage and sleeps well?

Though the Lord is on high, he looks upon the lowly.
Psalm 138:6

COMMON LIFE

Often in the car or crossing campus,
most recently on a plane to Charlotte,

the thought: *I don't want to leave all this.*
Not the broad arc of flight or even how

an airline attendant and a father feel
the same thing—say, the tremble of a wing

at thirty-two thousand feet—differently,
and neither is incorrect. *So, are you*

afraid to die? Klari asks on the way
back to school from an advisee dinner.

They are all under nineteen, my seven,
and it is Klari's sixteenth birthday.

For her present, I had let her pose me
any question. *Yes,* I say. *Me, too,* she says.

Search me, O God, and know my heart.
Psalm 139:23

DAVID SAYS

David says God
knows a word completely
even before
it passes into speech.

Every word. Not only
what it once meant
and means across all time zones
but how, too,

saying it—or not—
creates a future
we may—or may not—desire
or deserve.

David also says
this is how God knows him
and, by extension,
the rest of us:

as words forming
on history's broad tongue—from
unknown to knowing
to being known—

words wonderfully made:
musterion,
        eikon,
                euangelion.

The Lord secures justice for the poor and upholds the cause of the needy.
Psalm 140:12

AT THE ST. FRANCIS YACHT CLUB

To my left, Golden Gate; right, Alcatraz;
Sausalito, straight out across the bay.

Here protests are polite formalities
filed with a rotating race committee,

and I'm weak-kneed before Olympic gold,
framed press releases, action photos

of spinnakers, crews, square-jawed skippers.
Suffering here is elective, like prayer

or wondering what on earth St. Francis
would make of a yacht club that bears his name.

But I'm here for a wedding reception—
to *A-men* love and a nine-piece funk band—

and not to rule against the darling couple
in matching yellow rain slickers. Not now.

The wicked will learn that my words were well spoken.
Psalm 141:6

BLOOD

So, cuz, you ever think what's the use—this
writing thing—and feel like you wanna quit?

Kate and I trace a common bloodline
through a colonial home in Dedham.

Now I'm her creative writing teacher
at a chichi New England boarding school.

Sure, I answer. *Just this morning, in fact.*
Kate shifts in her seat. There are eleven

others at the table who do not know
what to do when we talk like this. Clearly

their parents are not shelling out tens
of thousands of dollars for their darlings

to eavesdrop on our familiar chit-chat.
She knows, too, I know it's not about writing.

When my spirit grows faint within me . . .
Psalm 142:3

RUMOR HAS IT

Religion is for the birds, she proclaimed
from the pulpit the week, by her own

initiative and at her own expense,
she had the sagging stained glass windows

removed and sent upstate for repairs.
Barely able to afford her, the congregation,

small, staid, and aging, hardly
recognized the smoke-darkened walls

as we choristers processed all wide-eyed
into thrilling light, a wind—not even

plastic over the empty frames—playing
among the pews, between legs, candle

fire jitterbugging on the altar. She led
worship that morning as though the life

of the world depended on our singing
those canticles and antiphons. Yes, hers

was my kind of spiritual madness—how
she took captive our deepest affections

and required of us laughter. Quite unlike
the bishop who, for her burial, ruled

that she be dressed in Eucharistic finery,
a faux-linen collar gripping her neck.

But he could not grant her the dying wish
she, all eyes at eighty-one, whispered

over whiskey to her funeral director—
to be buried "sans underwear"—who did.

May your good Spirit lead me.
Psalm 143:10

RETURNING

from a mid-winter retreat

Two white wooden lawn chairs the catalog calls
Adirondack pose side-by-side on the icy bank

of a small pond the locals call *Club Mud.*
Rising two miles behind, like a studio backdrop,

the face of the mountain we skied. This is Vermont
in February, the pond frozen, snow sitting

on everything but the lawn chairs because we
are sitting in them, Bill having just galumphed

from the camera on its tripod in the middle
of the pond. He has overcome sadness. Closing

on fifty and eager for the long drive home, he looks
as impish as I do. My contribution to the shot:

off to the side, like a winnowing fan planted
on a waterless plain, a black and yellow plastic oar.

Deliver me and rescue me.
Psalm 144:7

O MY SOUL

I thoroughly disgust me: my weakness,
smallness of mind, indifference to others'

little gains, painful losses; how I talk
of their lives in brief generalities,

reserve fascination for only mine: my field,
my barn, the rightness of my cause. Oh my soul,

have you heard? God has healing in his wings.
Or whatever was there—the broad effulgence

of a Father's love—that lifted Christ alive
from the grave, transfigured—yes—transformed.

Let every creature praise his holy name.
Psalm 145:21

PROCESSION

An unbroken line, more a river
      of starlings passed over the library
            courtyard, my fresh coffee going cold,

and just as it seemed the last
      pilgrim had straggled by, another wave,
            hundreds, no thousands more cleared

the treetops, streaming into view,
      their chatter ecstatic—for twenty minutes
            running—wave after wave after wave.

A bad day would make of them a figure
      for how *dismal* never seems to quit:
            word after word of shootings, suicides,

the heart's upwelling—felt as never ending—
      of raunch, revenge, temptations to silence
            conscience, do whatever damn well pleases.

But they are birds, not emblems.
      They did not arise from my dismal heart.
            They do not regard me as significant,

even less themselves. Their regard reserved
      for the ineffable *amen* moving in each
            that moves them all to join the long flight south.

The Lord sets prisoners free.
Psalm 146:7

IN THE HOSPITAL, BERRYMAN TO DYLAN

August 1966

I'm cross, idiot me, with god who has wrecked
this generation & your Triumph.
Is it so wrong to love another's machine? Oh,
Minnesota sends best wishes for your speedy
recovery. How convenient having god to be cross with,
the way I'm cross with what's-her-name

in New York, but neither here nor there. I am
easily crossed. Too easily seduced. & you—
look at you—look at me, sad prophets
of a hip & facile philosophy. But what if what's
wrecked weren't by god wrecked, what then? This
I know: birthed Kunitz was on the date your Triumph

failed you. & Mussolini. & Henry of Champagne.
Each hungry, cold, naked. Lately the feeling—
a better word, please?—that you there
in bed bruised, I still standing miraculous here, we
beyond complaint were made for praise. So,
where to start: you not gone, nor I. Nor yet Kunitz.

Make music to God on the harp.
Psalm 147:7

IN HEAVEN

CT: 277-TTT

St. Paul says we will judge angels. How odd
that work left to us. I would be happy

strumming a guitar, composing songs.
But if there are angels like the driver

of the smudge-grey gas guzzler I followed
this afternoon from Putnam to Pomfret—

who three times flung trash out the window, twice
flipped off random pedestrians, and yes,

winged something that exploded on my windshield—
I'm sure I'll relish judging angels.

For a season, anyway. And then after that
the pull of strings and new melodies

will return us all to the better work,
and good-for-nothing jerks will be no more.

The Lord's splendor is above the earth and the heavens.
Psalm 148:13

LIGHTNING, HAIL

Snail Darter and Ptarmigan, Walking Stick
and Platypus, everything that has breath

or makes breath possible—all wild grasses
and vines, pine forest and deciduous—

sun, moon, meteor, star, *praise ye the Lord,*
saith the psalmist as though—the absurdity

of this endearing—it were his job
to pronounce the cosmic imperative:

asteroid like a mountain that will slam
through earth's paper thin atmosphere, *praise Him.*

Praise His name with dancing, with tambourine and harp.
Psalm 149:3

TOWARD A NEW SONG

This rain, a nor'easter, is nothing new.
Within a week—sunlight over the wide,

redding forest—the playing fields will dry
and our teams finish out their seasons.

Then term will end, the dining hall empty,
and by the time I am done drafting

these poems, Bill will be married again.
For my friend's new life, I am thankful.

For the rhythms of this work and art's long
obedience, thankful. Soon enough:

seasonal obligations, last minute shopping.
For now, I am thankful for how all things

seem to resolve into song—and the high call
to bend our wills to set a wronged world right.

Let everything that has breath praise the Lord.
Psalm 150:6

SHONDA-LA

*I would rather speak five intelligible words to instruct others
than ten thousand in some ecstatic tongue.*
1 Corinthians 14:19

Do you breathe? Praise God.

Notes

Regarding epigraphs and biblical quotations: I borrow/adapt chiefly from the New International Version of the Bible, showing occasional deference to the King James Version and The Psalter in the *Book of Common Prayer*.

Psalm 1   *Ashre* is Hebrew for "blessed" or "happy." The italicized lines are from the psalm, though I take modest liberties. Had the car been an older model, it would have been totaled.

Psalm 5   "Moto" (as in Moto Guzzi) is the name of a favorite café-restaurant under the elevated JMZ subway line on the border between the Latino and Hassidic neighborhoods of South Williamsburg. As is the case in many of these poems, this one contains echoes of several New Testament passages: Philippians 4:8, Revelation 21:1–4, Philippians 2:6–11.

Psalm 7   *Narcissus poeticus* is the name of a small, white, aromatic daffodil I have always known as the paperwhite. Again, a New Testament echo: Revelation 8:1–5.

Psalm 8   In *Paradise Lost*, the descent of Milton's Satan to earth by way of the celestial spheres culminates in his lighting vulture-like on a tree in Eden. Purely fanciful, Milton's description makes cinematic the unseen entrance of that deceitful shape-shifter into the human experience.

Psalm 11   The biblical book of Esther, though hardly funny, is a classic comedy: in the end, the bad guy (Haman) gets the misery he planned for the good guy (Mordecai), and the good guy gets the glory the bad guy had intended for himself.

Psalm 12   The italicized words are from Philippians 2:9–13 (New Testament), and the Hopkins line about Christ being the just critic is lifted from poem

"10" of Berryman's "Eleven Addresses to the Lord" in *Love & Fame* (Farrar, Straus & Giroux, 1970).

Psalm 16   "turning onto campus" In 1986, I moved onto the grounds of a boarding school. Since then, all trips home have been toward and back onto campus.

Psalm 19   "the fire that burns yet will not consume them" cf. Exodus 3:1–6.

Psalm 21   "like the Spirit above the primal sea" cf. Genesis 1:1–2.

Psalm 22   "numbered among the conflicted" is meant to echo the messianic prophesy in Isaiah 53:12 regarding the Suffering Servant: "he was numbered among the transgressors." The italicized last line is my summary of the psalm's last six verses, with a nod to Psalm 8.

Psalm 24   Line 11 is a conflation of Psalm 22:27 and Psalm 24:10. Line 14 is from Psalm 24:1.

Psalm 25   The quotation in lines 4 and 5 is from John Calvin's *Institutes of the Christian Religion* (Book II, Chapter 2, Section 18) published by Eerdmans (1972).

Psalm 26   "prone to wander" is from the hymn, "Come, Thou Font of Every Blessing," words by Robert Robinson (1758). The quotation in the final couplet is from 1 Peter 4:8.

Psalm 30   "divine shook-foil glimmer" cf. G. M. Hopkins' "God's Grandeur," line 2; his influence is everywhere in me if not in the poems.

Psalm 33   "the New Earth" cf. Revelation 21:1.

Psalm 34   The Hebrew psalm is an acrostic; the verses begin with successive letters of the alphabet. Each line of my poem does the same.

Psalm 36   "powers and principalities" In biblical theology, the nations and all earthly institutions are understood as being players in humanity's rebellion against the sovereignty of God. This rebellion is fed by both human sinfulness and, as the 1979 *Book of Common Prayer* (p. 302) says, "Satan and all the spiritual forces of wickedness that rebel against God." In the New Testament, "powers and principalities" may be understood as angelic orders that rank very highly among these spiritual forces. "Mordor" is, of course, J. R. R. Tolkien's hellish invention in *The Lord of the Rings*. A "Telecaster" is a Fender electric guitar (and my axe of choice).

Psalm 40   "the notch" is Smugglers Notch. That far north in Vermont, the Long Trail is more primitive and rigorous than we expected.

Psalm 43   *Musterion tes anomias* "Mystery of lawlessness" From St. Paul's second letter to believers in Thessalonica (2:7) where he notes the mystery is pitted against truth yet under extraordinary temporary restraint.

Psalm 45   "Silly Sally" is the name of a word game. The rule is observed in the poem.

Psalm 51   Eleanor "Aunt El" Vandevort: friend, mentor, sister, former missionary in the Sudan.

Psalm 54   "Vengeance is mine" Deuteronomy 32:35 and Romans 12:19

Psalm 55   "Angel with a bowl" From perhaps the saddest chapter in all the Christian scriptures: Revelation 16.

Psalm 57   Mary's Magnificat from Luke 1:46–55.

Psalm 63   Woodstock Fair: a large, late-summer, agricultural fair in Woodstock (CT) that features a wildly diverse performance series.

Psalm 66   "Foxes have holes and birds of the air have nests" Matthew 8:20.

Psalm 67   Many of the biblical psalms (all of which were and, in some circles, still are sung with instrumentation) include cryptic rubrics addressed to a director of music. In this poem, the director of music is God.

Psalm 69   "*Selah*" An untranslatable Hebrew word, perhaps a musical term.

Psalm 71   In the instant before his fall from those reservoir rocks in Wilton (CT), Jerry shoved to safety a friend who had lost her balance and was stumbling toward the cliff's edge. "No greater love" (John 15:13).

Psalm 72   Often when biblical writers have glimpsed God's *pathos* (A. J. Heschel, *The Prophets*, Harper & Row, 1969)—peace, justice, mercy, love, judgment, compassion—they describe its force as a surging river or irrepressible flood.

Psalm 73   *poiema* (a word that inclines toward "masterpiece") is lifted from the New Testament letter to the Ephesians (2:10) where it refers directly to the community for whom it was written ("we are God's *poiema*") and indirectly to all humanity. The inclusion of "all things" leans on Genesis 1 and 2: "God saw all that he had made, and it was very good."

Psalm 76   In Genesis 22, God commands in order to call off, once for all, a hideous religious ritual: the sacrifice of firstborn sons. In Luke 22, Jesus prohibits violence as a means of preventing a hideous political ritual: the elimination of the (merely and/or urgently) unwanted.

Psalm 81   "right mind" is a Buddhist virtue also referring to the state of mind (and soul and spirit) to which a demoniac named Legion was restored following his healing by Jesus (Luke 8:26–39).

Psalm 89   "wars and rumors of wars" are regarded by Jesus as part of the normal historical context preceding "the end" when "the Son of Man comes in the clouds with great power and glory" (Mark 13). Of them he says, "Do not be alarmed" (verse 7). The pelican is a traditional symbol for Christ.

Psalm 91   The final couplet attempts a contrast of the Bible's old and new order attitudes toward the enemies of God's good purposes (cf. Psalm 91:8 and 2 Peter 3:9).

Psalm 92   "unicorn"—peculiar that the King James Version translates the Hebrew word *reem* as "unicorn." The NIV has "wild ox."

Psalm 93   "comfortable in Zion" is a phrase borrowed from the prophet Amos (Amos 6:1ff.) who railed against those who, in their fine houses, claimed to be religious but, immersed in their comfortable lives, neglected the poor. "*The Lord reigns*" is the opening declaration in Psalm 93. The other quotations are from 1 John 4:16, pop-religious culture, and Job 1:21, each of which has been often misused as a springboard to the denial or devaluation of genuine struggle and suffering. The poem participates in the biblical tradition of lamentation (e.g., the entire Old Testament book called "Lamentations" and, in the New Testament, Matthew 5:4; Luke 19:41; John 11:32–36; and 16:19–22) wherein grief is deep and fully felt, yet sufferers also know a hope that will not finally disappoint.

Psalm 94   "pay back" This notion (cf. Psalm 94:1–2, 23) connects with the eschatological expectation that, come the Day of the Lord, the haughty oppressor will be brought low and the humble oppressed will be exalted (Luke 1:46–55).

Psalm 95   The white horse and rider were not invented for the poem; they were there that day. The little girl, on the other hand, may not have been; I don't remember. She may simply have become necessary as the poem developed (pardon the pun). In the "nose to nose" moment of the poem, a conflation of biblical images: (1) the mounted, conquering Messiah in Revelation 19:11ff. and (2) all creation, personified in the little girl, thrilling at the arrival of the long expected Jesus (Romans 8:18–25). Certainly Donna lived and died in this hope.

Psalm 96   The opening quotation is drawn from the poem's triggering psalm (verses 10 and 11). The debate over the bodily resurrection of Jesus is not an invention of modern scholarship; the apostle Paul, in his first letter to the Corinthians, dedicates considerable ink and parchment to the controversy (chapter 15) and concludes that if the body of Jesus was not raised as the gospels declare then the entire Christian thing collapses utterly and "believers" are fools most to be pitied. The modern deliteralization of the word "resurrection" (reduced to a synonym for renewal) is the product of a worldview unable to accept that the power of God changed and raised the human body of Jesus, making it a spiritual body that both retains continuity with his physical body and transcends it. Indeed, the resurrection of Jesus may very well have been the single most outlandish event in human history. Think Big Bang of a New Creation. So much depends on who one thinks Jesus was; consider John 1:1–14; Colossians 1:15ff.; and Hebrews 1:3. Finally, "thief-thick Paradise" alludes to Jesus' conversation with the criminal who died on a cross along side his (Luke 23:32–43).

Psalm 97   The David and Goliath story is found in 1 Samuel 17.

Psalm 98   "a father's well-prepared welcome home" refers to a parable in Luke's gospel (Luke 15:11–24). That which "never fails to spoil our truest effort" is human sinfulness (1 John 1:8–9).

Psalm 99   "nonattachment"—a Buddhist ideal that has a Christian analog: Luke 12:13–31.

Psalm 101   "What bath / to restore the good dream?" This is not a veiled allusion to the practice of baptism. Baptism is an act of identification, inclusion, and hope that anticipates an inner cleansing but does not effect it. Two beatitudes of Jesus come to mind: "Blessed are those who hunger and thirst for righteousness" and "Blessed are the pure in heart"—for the hungry will be filled and the pure will see God (Matthew 5:6, 8).

Psalm 102   The owl and the ashes are images borrowed from the poem's triggering psalm: verses 6 and 9. In the poem, the owl has become an emblem of the divine and how the divine is present in the least likely of environs.

Psalm 103   The quotations in this poem are drawn from the psalm, verses 1 and 20–22, respectively.

Psalm 104   Reading this psalm, I enjoyed a moment's feel for how, before the fall (thus, "In the early chapters" of Genesis), all things, all creatures, and humanity existed peaceably in the perfect pleasure of the creator: the earth "like a bride," humanity like adornments selected for the bridegroom's delight.

Psalm 105   Though in the spirit of Psalm 104, this poem was launched by the phrase in 105:5, "Remember the wonders he has done." Whereas the psalmist takes forty-plus verses to recall a few of God's wonders, my "short list" requires only four, five including the title. And, yes, human desire and the good things that desire hath wrought are among the wonders of God's handiwork and participate in his grand *poiema*.

Psalm 106   *pornea* (impurity) is anything that works against the grain of God's *poiema* and the "future" God intends for humanity and all creation (Jeremiah 29:11).

Psalm 107   As well as being a photographer, Bill is a professional musician whose instrument-of-choice is the pedal steel guitar. "Blues Junior" is an amplifier I play my Tele through.

Psalm 112   After having hung with the likes of Ginsberg, Ferlinghetti, Olson, and Snyder in NYC during the early Sixties, poet Drum Hadley moved west to become a cowboy. Since then he has continued to write and publish, winning a coveted Spur Award in 2006. He has also become a champion of grasslands conservation in the Southwest through his work with the Animas Foundation and the Malpai Borderlands Group (malpaiborder-landsgroup.org). A "cutting horse" is one trained for herding and, in Drum's experience, going after livestock lost in arroyo canyons.

Psalm 113   A drop to third boat would be from a varsity to a junior varsity boat.

Psalm 114   Theophanies are usually accompanied by dramatic earthly effects.

Psalm 115   A persona poem: an unnamed singer-songwriter. A "green room" is the backstage room where a performer prepares for and unwinds from a gig. "The door" is the total cash received for admission to the gig. And yes, "a sunless sea" is from Coleridge's "Kubla Khan."

Psalm 116   In biblical theology, the wage paid to sin (*harmatia*, meaning "miss the mark" or "err") is death (Genesis 2:15–17; Romans 6:23), a spiritual experience that finds its physical analog in the process of dying.

Psalm 117   This poem is a serious frolic, thus "gambol." "Light of Light, very God of very God" is from the Nicene Creed. Also, cf., Hebrews 11:6.

Psalm 119   cf., Luke 8:26–39, especially verse 35.

Psalm 120   Kedar, a grandson of Abraham, developed something of a bad "rep" in ancient Israel. "Tents of Kedar" is a metaphor for the Presidency of him whose visit to Georgia precipitated a thin veneer of urban renewal in Tbilisi.

Psalm 122   The "one philosopher" is Ernest Nagel. "A better country" is from Hebrews 11.

Psalm 124   "lived and moved and knew my shirt size" borrows from Acts 17:28 where Paul, speaking of God to Athenians, quotes from a poem by the Cretan poet Epimenides: "in whom we live and move and have our being."

Psalm 126   A life of service is one way to bear witness to what is right and good. "Herod's goons in Bedlam" refers to the slaughter of the innocents recorded in Matthew 2.

Psalm 127   Another persona poem: an unnamed soldier standing guard over an ancient city.

Psalm 128   *Philia*—Brother-love.

Psalm 129   Perhaps you, too, have experienced religious ritual so dull that you easily imagine all heaven sneaking mischievously out the back.

Psalm 134   Richard Speck was a mass murderer from Chicago whose story in the Sixties was the first of its kind to be covered on television.

Psalm 139   *Musterion*: mystery. *Eikon*: image. *Euangelion*: good news.

Psalm 142   Yet another persona poem: an unnamed parishioner in an unnamed parish.

Psalm 143   "A winnowing fan planted on a waterless plain" alludes to Teiresias' advice to Odysseus, after dispensing with the suitors, to bear an oar inland until someone asks what manner of winnowing-fan it is.

Psalm 146   An invented situation, shortly after Dylan's near-fatal motorcycle accident. The opening two lines incorporate something Berryman wrote somewhere: "I'm cross with god who has wrecked this generation." The idea for the poem arrived by way of David Wojahn's "rock and roll sonnets" in *Mystery Train* (University of Pittsburgh, 1990).

Psalm 147   "judging angels," cf. 1 Corinthians 3:6.

Psalm 150   "Shonda-La" may echo faintly and with good humor Eliot's "shanti, shanti, shanti" from "The Wasteland," but in circles I've traveled, "shonda-la" is often merely a series of nonsense syllables used good-naturedly to mimic the sound of someone speaking or praying in "tongues" (glossolalia), an outward lingual sign of an inward ecstatic grace.